OPEN BOOK

OPEN BOOK

Little Thoughts from a Big Head

MIKE BULLARD

Seal Books

Seal Books and colophon are trademarks of Random House of Canada Limited

OPEN BOOK
Seal Books/published by arrangement with Doubleday Canada
Doubleday hardcover edition published 1999
Seal Books edition published June 2000

ISBN: 0-7704-2842-8

Seal Books are published by Doubleday Canada, a division of Random House of Canada Limited. "Seal Books" and the portrayal of a seal, are the property of Random House of Canada Limited, Toronto, Ontario.

Cover photograph by Edward Gajdel
Cover design by Susan Thomas / Digital Zone
Text design by Heidy Lawrance Associates

Printed and bound in Canada

TRAN 10 9 8 7 6 5 4 3 2 1

*To my family because I love them
and because studies indicate that
you sell more books this way.*

*And to the believers at CTV
because I'm not stupid.*

OPEN BOOK

OPEN LETTER

Okay, so some of the readers of this book are also its writers. They are the thousands of fans who write the show every day with questions, comments, and suggestions. And every day JeniB (yes, from *JeniB* magazine) writes them back. And every so often we get complaints that I am too busy to answer my own e-mail, which is accurate. I am too busy to answer all of them. But I do read some, the writers read some, and the producers sit on their fat asses and read the rest while our own JeniB answers them all. We apologize that JeniB is not present in this book, but to tell you the truth, she's sick of all of you. Don't take it personally. She's sick of me too!

When my editor, Maya Mavjee, approached me with the idea of doing a book, I agreed but felt uncomfortable writing an essay-style humour book. I'm not into humour. I'm a comedian. That's when Al Magee, my oldest friend and producer and co-creator of *Open Mike* and all-round know-it-all, suggested that we simply answer the e-mail. I hated that he suggested it almost as much as I liked the idea. But eventually I had to admit that it was perfect. That way our fans and those strange people who hate the show but who continue to watch will have their e-mail answered. And I had half my book written for me by you. But no complaints. I do not want JeniB to have to respond to even one whiny complaint about what we did to your e-mail. Here are a list of things we did and why we did them. If you don't like it, e-mail some other show and complain to them.

1. We left out people's last names for legal reasons.

2. We couldn't answer every e-mail. So we tried to pick ones that represented the thoughts of many. We're sorry if you had the same question or idea and your name doesn't appear.

3. Some e-mails were edited for length or because they were repetitive or just had irrelevant information or had too-relevant information or because they were obscene or because they were just too long and boring. That's just the kind of people we are.

4. We tried to leave the spelling and punctuation as it was, but it was tough. The editors don't like it. As a special gift to them I'm letting them give you all a little grammar lesson here. Take it away, Maya.

A Note from the Editor

While we realize that e-mail culture is stylistically iconoclastic and that correct grammar and spelling are considered "square," I have to make a few suggestions. A refresher, if you will.

"You're" means "You are." It is not possessive.

"Its" is possessive (i.e., The cat chased its tail). It's means "it is."

Orin is spelled exactly like that. Not Oryn. Not Irin. And certainly not Irwin.

Thank you Mike. I feel much better.
Maya

FOREWORD

by Mike Bullard as told to his faithful dog,
Yankee, using a DH10 Voice Recorder

Writing a book, on any subject, is a hard, stress-filled process. It occupies your every waking moment. It alienates you from your friends and loved ones. It can cause anxiety attacks, even loss of fur. Er ... hair. This book you are sniffing is the culmination of my innermost thoughts and feelings. I have plumbed the depths of my soul and tried to answer the questions that haunt us all: Who are we? Why are we here? Why do we have to go outside to do our business while cats get to use a box in the laundry room? Heady stuff for a talk show host, I admit.

Speaking of talk shows, I guess it's no secret I owe my present success to *Open Mike*. To think it began only a little over two years ago (it seems so much longer, like, say, seven years.) My agent told me that the fledgling Comedy Network wanted me to host its flagship production: an hour-long comedy, variety, and talk program. You can imagine my happiness. I was so excited, I was jumping up and down on total strangers, knocking stuff off the end tables, scaring children. I knew right there and then that this show would be unlike any other talk show in Canadian television history: It would be passably good. Opportunity was scratching at the door and it was just a question of whether I was going to let it in because the kitchen floor had just been waxed. I had a feeling. Call it intuition. Call it kismet. Call it worms.

I knew this show was going to say something to the Canadian viewing public, something positive and uplifting, which was good. And if they had their TVs on to see it, even better.

When the editors at Doubleday asked me to write a book I was hesitant at first. When they told me how much it paid, hesitance turned to outright reluctance. Besides, I was afraid of failing. What if the book wasn't any good? But then I thought, "Hey, what am I worried about? Writing a book is easy. It's just taking the stuff inside you and putting it on paper." And I've been "putting it on paper" for years. And as far as failing, what's wrong with that? You just pick yourself up, lick yourself off, and start over. So I accepted the offer and I'm proud to say that the tome you are now holding in your mouth ... make that hands ... represents the best I have to offer. Combine that with the fact you probably found the thing in the remainder bin and you've got yourselves a sweet little deal.

I hope you enjoy reading this book as much as I enjoyed writing it.

Bark! Bark!

ON FAN MAIL

Before we get too far into this book I thought I'd include a note on my fans and their e-mail. There are several stylistic choices to be made when writing a fan letter. Here are examples of some of the categories of people who continue to send me e-mails.

The Enthusiast

Enthusiasts are just that. They like to tell you that they like you, that they think you are doing a good job, and that they will continue to support you. These are the ideal fans, and yet, like a girl who likes you in grade six, it seems suspiciously easy. There must be something wrong with them. Who sits and writes a letter just because they like you?

The Agenda Fan

These fans disguise themselves as enthusiasts but always give themselves away near the end of the letter when they slip in a request for a job, money, or a personal appearance. Often these fans are in, or know someone who has, a band.

The Encourager

Encouragers almost like you but have a couple of complaints. They want to tell you where you are going wrong, but they recognize that it's a hard job and they want to encourage you to improve. They are like a mother who admires her daughter's dress and then picks a bit of lint off the shoulder. "There. Now you're perfect."

The Angry Fan

These fans hate you so much they feel compelled to sit down and write out every thing they find despicable about you. For some reason, these fans are particularly loyal and tend to write often.

The Discourager

Discouragers have no particular complaints; they just want to let you know that they think you are doing a lousy job. They are too passive to hate and too lazy to change the channel. They have only enough energy to fire off a missive describing their particular dissatisfactions.

The Comparison Shopper

These are the people who like to remind you that you are nowhere near as good as your American counterpart, that you will never be as good as your American counterpart, and that, in fact, you shouldn't even bother trying. In previous years these fans were simply called The Canadians, but in recent years there has been a mass defection from this category, hence the renaming.

Hey, Mike: Do people ask you stupid questions now that you're famous?

DEREK, BRAMPTON, ONTARIO

Why, yes, Derek, they do.

1. If I've heard it once, I've heard it a thousand times: "You're bigger off TV." Makes sense to me; most people have a 29" TV at most. Hammy Hamster is bigger off television than on it. Well, wait — bad example.

2. It is not a great compliment to a talk show host when you walk up to him and say, "You're a great actor."

Hey, Mike: What things do guests say that you would rather not hear?

ANONYMOUS

There are only four things that really worry me:

1. "I've brought you something." I don't like props and, to me, presents are props. Now, off-screen is a different matter. Shower me with presents; see if I care.

2. Just before the show each night I go into the green room and meet the guests. I always cringe when I shake their hands and they say, "Man, I'm tired." Fills me with confidence, that one does.

3. "I've never seen the show." That bugs the hell out of me. Even in the beginning, when no one had seen the show, that bugged me. It even bugs me when Americans say it.

4. "You made fun of my wife once in a club." Too cryptic. I don't know if the guy liked it or didn't like it. And I don't want to find out when we're on the air.

Hey, Mike: How did you lose your virginity?

MARY

How I Lost My Virginity

She was thirty-nine. (For legal reasons, I'll call her Dave.) I was twenty. (For comedy's sake, I'll call myself handsome.) And we met about a mile away from her house. I'd just returned from the Yukon, where I'd been working in a silver mine. It seemed like everybody was working in mines back then. I came home and my brother's girlfriend's older sister had a friend who was getting a divorce. We met at a party and it was instant chemistry. I used to jog back then. I put on my track suit. It seemed like everybody wore track suits back then. And I'd leave the house Monday morning and come home Friday night. I told my dad that I was training for the Iron Man contest. My father, who is kind of purposely naïve and who doesn't like to hear about sexual matters, believed me. She is now sixty-one, and I'm pretty sure that if I saw her now, those old feelings wouldn't come flooding back.

Hey, Mike: I saw you jogging down Yonge Street. You looked real tired. Since when did you start exercising?

DANIELLE N.

I make no bones about the fact I'm no athlete. Blame my father. We were never pushed into sports when we were kids. When most Canadian kids were learning how to skate, my dad was in the backyard with a garden hose freezing us a talk show set. It's all fun and games until somebody's tongue gets frozen to the desk mike. Of course, when there wasn't any snow we'd set furniture up in the street and play. I ended a lot of my earlier interviews by screaming, "Car!" Still do.

Hey, Mike: I was just wondering how you got your big break, because the first time I saw you, you were on the Comedy Network with crappy guests. Now you have a new channel with good guests. What happened?

JENNIFER S., CAPE BRETON, N.S.

I'll tell you one thing that didn't get better when we moved to the new channel: the quality of the e-mails we receive. Clean up the language, Jennifer, or you won't be in my next book.

To answer your question: CTV ran out of late movies and we ran out of Celtic bands. The first season at Gretzky's was an opportunity to learn the craft of hosting a talk show without the pretence of a huge network audience, a huge studio audience, or a working thermostat. (Just for the record, we found Gretzky's to be a terrific place to do the show. The location was great, the staff was friendly, and we'd still be there if it wasn't for the asbestos.)

Unfortunately, celebrities on the talk show circuit don't bother to stop where the viewership is too small. So while Dini Petty continued to snag the likes of Phil Collins and Robert Duvall, I had to cut my interviewing teeth on aspiring Ashley MacIsaacs (we still haven't got the real Ashley). I don't like to brag, but our streak of forty-one consecutive shows in which some if not all of the guests were Celtic bands remains a record for non-Irish television. It was vital training because even the better guests in Canada have no talk show experience, so it's rare that I can count on anyone to carry a segment the way Tom Hanks or Billy Crystal would. The upside is that with no talk show experience, our guests don't know to complain when we pick them up at the hotel in a rickshaw.

After our first ten weeks on the Comedy Network, CTV decided that we were ready for a trial run at 12:35 a.m. We've been in that slot ever since, much to the dismay of movie-lovers, who have to wait an extra hour to see *Eddie and the Cruisers 2*. Now that we have access to the broad network audience, the likes of Jewel and John Mellencamp see fit to drop by. Sadly, they'll never return because they inevitably find the rickshaw uncomfortable.

Hey, Mike: You shot for a whole year in Wayne Gretzky's restaurant and he didn't even come on your show. What gives?

ROBERT N.

Well, he came to the show once, but all he did was stand against the wall watching us for half an hour. He also refused to appear in a taped remote. But I don't think it's shyness, because he's been on Letterman about nineteen times.

Hey, Mike: When are you going to open a restaurant?

FRANK M., VANCOUVER

Well, this might be a good time to mention that I find the whole idea of celebrity-themed restaurants ridiculous. What's the logic of these things? Do people think: "I like the way this guy passes a hockey puck so I certainly would like to eat in a restaurant in which he has a small financial interest." It's not like you're going to run into the celebrity there. The times Gretzky was around, the restaurant was closed to the public and there were bouncers posted around the entrances. I think one of them was Dave Semenko.

Hey, Mike: Why do you hate kids so much?

J.L.

Why do I hate kids so much, with their backwards base-ball hats, huge pants with room for three worn no higher than the thigh, earrings and studs pierced through any piece of flesh that dangles, bumming money from Mom and Dad for a pair of Nikes that'll never set foot on a court, smarting off to any adult who suggests they look ridiculous? Why do I hate 'em?

'Cause it's a look I can't get away with.

Let me tell you a little story.

I was on tour a couple of years back, and when you're on the road you've got to find things to fill in the days. I find that going to the local mall to cause trouble works best. There are always plenty of kids and they're usually without their parents. In a mall in London one time, one of the other comics and I spent the day stealing hats off of kids' heads and running away. There's not much to the game. It's simple, but the look of shock that comes over their faces is worth getting your name written down in the mall security book. I grabbed this one kid's hat and then went to a movie. When we came out of the mall, the kid was standing there with about eight or nine friends. They were all about four feet tall except for this one guy who looked about 5'8". Well, I didn't want to take any chances, as I had to do a show that night. So we ran. The head of security stopped us on our way out and took our names and addresses. I gave him the head-liner's name. When we got back to the hotel, the cops were at his door. I won't say his name but he was still drunk from the night before and apologized for taking the kid's hat. It doesn't exactly answer your question, but it was fun.

Hey, Mike: My mom says that you look like a Cabbage Patch kid. I tried to defend you but she beat me. Please help me; can I come live with you?

GOLAUSON

Please see previous entry.

Hey, Mike: When will you ever make a show with a clean shave?

VINNY, OTTAWA

Excellent question, my friend, although I find it hard to believe that anyone named "Vinny" has been clean-shaven a day in his life. The truth is, I would love to do the show each night with a fresh shave, but I made a promise to the network.

Even though my contract prohibits me from using a razor, thanks to computer enhancement technology, I can show you what it would look like.

After Computer Enhancement

As you can see, I'd be out of the network's price range.

Hey, Mike: How come you get more applause than laughter in your show? Thought I'd ask.

ASHLEY A., PRINCE ALBERT, SASKATCHEWAN

Ever since Bob Dylan played the Masonic Temple in 1996, the place has been infested with gnats and flies. Until we have time to fumigate, you're going to hear more relentless clapping whether or not the show deserves it.

Having said that, there isn't a talk show on television that doesn't have the noise of unwarranted applause. I think audiences have been conditioned to applaud from watching other shows. People assume we have an applause sign, partly because I've joked on the air about having one, but we really don't. And we don't sweeten. That's the fancy-ass term for adding canned laughter. Which is the techie term for laughtrack.

I also think our audience frequently applauds the monologue jokes because they can sense what an ordeal it is for me to do written material. It's like clapping for the guy who finishes last in the New York City Marathon — they respect the fact that he ignored the intense pain to get to the finish line. One of these days I'm going to collapse in the middle of a joke. Unfortunately, that'll get a bigger laugh than the material ever got.

Question: Has anyone there heard of a radio show from the mid-sixties called "Open Mike?" It was based out of Halifax ... CHNS, I think. The reason I ask is because "Open Mike" was the name of my father's radio show and it is kind of neat to see the phrase used again ... especially for a show of this calibre. Really impressive. Keep up the good work. I am sure my father would have enjoyed it.

MICHAEL M.

This is preposterous. The phrase "Open Mike" was invented by me and Comedy Network VP Ed Robinson during an all-night brainstorming session in October 1997. Every once in a while we get these ridiculous claims. It's no big deal — our lawyers go to court and annihilate people like your father about fifteen times a year.

For you trivia buffs, here are some other show titles seriously bandied about by the Comedy Network before we settled on *Open Mike*:

- *Insulting the Crowd and Ignoring the Guests with Mike Bullard*
- *The Canadian Tonight Show*
- *This Hour Has 22 Pretty Good Minutes*
- *There's Something About Mikey*
- *Forced Applause with Mike Bullard*
- *The Alan Thicke Show without Alan Thicke*
- *The Squinting Hour*
- *After M*A*S*H*
- *The Show Pat Bullard Turned Down*

17

Hey, Mike: I've been watching your show for a while now, and I was wondering how come on every e-mail night you only use e-mails from people that compliment your show. Why don't you put on some that make fun of your show, so you get big laughs? Believe me, it will work.

A BIG FAN, DONALD S., TRAIL, B.C.

What if it doesn't work, Don? Are you going to make everything right again? Sure, you can make any far-out promise you want, knowing that if things blow up in our faces, you're three thousand kilometres away. Go to hell.

Hey, Mike: Hi, just wondering if the show accepts unsolicited bits? I'm breaking into the writing field and know I can do better than some of the stuff Mike's doing!

THANKS, MARK

Our writers are three of the best this country has produced. If you can do better than they can, then I'm surprised I haven't already heard of you, fired you, or turned you down already.

We've gotten hundreds of e-mails about how much the writers suck. Their own parents think they suck. The reason people think they suck is that I've always been a spontaneous comedian, and I like delivering written material as much as Wayne Gretzky likes delivering bodychecks — it's just never been a part of my game. As a result, I'll downplay the written joke in favour of audience interplay. Often I'll start talking to the audience in the middle of a written joke. My writers say that if I was Henny Youngman, I would do his signature bit like this: "Take my wife ... Hi, sir, where are you from? Well, that explains the ox parked outside ... please." Perhaps you've noticed that sometimes I'll mumble a written joke so it can't be understood (my apologies to the closed caption typists) while my ad libs are always clearly audible.

Realizing early on that I'm probably going to live or die by my ad libs, I created an adversarial scenario in which it appears I've been *forced* to do the written material. This attitude turns the audience against the jokes, therefore ensuring they tank most of the time. Then I seem all the more heroic when I "bail out" the monologue with improvisation. Obviously, no writers are going to shine under these circumstances. That's why a joke on our show might be described as "lame," while the same joke on *This Hour Has 22 Minutes* would be described as "brilliant."

But take heart, Mark, because my constant mangling of the written material will undoubtedly lead to writer resignations and suicides, opening up positions for new writers. And more good news, Mark: We've decided that these new writers will not be up-and-coming writer/comedians who've come to our attention by causing a stir in the industry ... they'll be strangers who e-mail us.

Hey, Mike: Hey, I saw you do some stand-up and you were pretty damn funny, and now you're not funny on your show. Is it because of the writers?
ERIC H.

Yes, it's because of the writers. I wish they'd stop forcing me to do that scripted junk and let me be myself. Where are you from, Eric? Well, that explains the ox parked outside.

Hey, Mike the man: I love your show, and I was just wondering aren't you scared standing so close to the audience when you're doing your monologue? Don't you ever think that someone in the front row can punch you right in the groin and you wouldn't even suspect it?

YOUR CANADIAN PAL, ANDREW S.,

NEWOLDTOWN, ALBERTA

I'm not concerned about the audience, because I'm facing them and can see if anyone is coming at me. It's the band I'm worried about.

But if something's going to happen, it's going to happen. I'd be more concerned if I was Juliette Powell, the woman who hosts *Electric Circus* — she's in the middle of her insane audience. I can't believe she stands there saying things like "The party is just heating up" instead of "I'm terrified" or "We're in way over our heads tonight." I'm pretty sure they've got her tethered to something so the crowd can't walk away with her — that's how the original host, Monika Deol, disappeared.

People assume there's way more security in this world than there really is. They think it would be hard to punch a celebrity, they think they'll get caught jumping the subway turnstile, they think the police give a damn if their car is stolen. Listen to me, Andrew: If someone can throw a pie in Bill Gates's face, people can do anything. There's a giant electric fence and armed guards protecting the White House, and yet any girl in a beret can get into the Oval Office and memorize the launch codes while the president is talking on the phone.

For the cost of a flimsy Canadian book, here's the big secret of life: The entire world works on the honour system. If you want to go to a movie without paying, you can. Just walk in when it's crowded while the usher is busy teaching a senior citizen how to work the straw dispenser. If you don't want to pay taxes, make up phony businesses and claim everything you own as a deduction. I know so many people who don't pay taxes. Perhaps you've met them — they're the ones always whining about the cutbacks at hospitals and schools.

Luckily, most Canadians aren't like that. Otherwise, it'd be a total mess like Russia or Somalia. I estimate only one out of ten Canadians is freeloading, so we have a prosperous and functioning society. But if you want to be the one out of ten, by all means keep reading this book until the end while you stand there in the book-store, then put it back on the shelf.

And if you *are* in the bookstore, do yourself a favour and go to the section where they have the books about movies. There's something called the *Roger Ebert Home Video Companion*, or something like that. Because it's updated with new movies every year, it keeps getting bigger and bigger and now it's the fattest book on the whole shelf. Normally, I don't derive humour from people's physical shortcomings, other than my own, but isn't there something funny about Roger Ebert having the fattest book on the shelf?

Hey, Mike: What have you got against cats?

JEBODIAH, JUNIUS, NFLD

They killed my sister.

Hey, Mike: Hockey is a national pastime and you are a national icon, and yet you don't like hockey. Very confusing.

DARLENE, TIMMINS, ONTARIO

It'll be a lot less confusing in a few years when basketball becomes the most popular sport in Canada. I went looking for hockey equipment for my son and found that it costs a couple of thousand dollars, and that they grow out of the stuff every year and you've got to spend the money all over again. All that for a sport with a severe risk of injury, practice times as early as 5 a.m., and coaches who are making up for a lack of authority in their lives by screaming profanities at eleven-year-olds. You hear all the time about what a great dad Walter Gretzky was to make all of those sacrifices for Wayne, but people should remember that his son was scoring three hundred goals a season. Try driving through a blizzard at 5 a.m. when your son plays only if the rest of the team gets the chicken pox.

Basketball, which I also don't follow, has no equipment and much less violence than hockey. From what I can tell, it also has far fewer morons involved. No wonder parents are steering their kids away from hockey. It's an especially easy decision for immigrants who fled their home countries because the streets were governed by rules similar to those in hockey. In cities like Toronto, where ten percent of the population arrived in Canada after 1990, and the majority have been here for less than thirty years, it's pretty clear that the domination of hockey is winding down. It'll hang on, the way the *Tommy Hunter Show* hung on, but it will end eventually.

But I got turned off hockey long before I was a hockey parent. When I was young, most of the kids in my neighbourhood couldn't afford fancy equipment for shinny hockey. Instead of shin pads, everyone used magazines. But instead of sending me out with the Sears catalogue or even *Saturday Night*, my mom made me wear *Flare* and *Cosmopolitan*. She thought the glossy covers afforded more protection, which they did, but the other kids' mockery left scars where the magazines could not protect: my heart.

SO, YOU WANT TO SIT IN THE CHAIR...

Over the last year, I've watched over four hundred people take the seat beside me. Some have thrived; others were mesmerized by the monitor. But from the first guest to last night's show, I marvel at the talk show format. It is unlike any other medium. Why? Because talk shows are not really talk shows. They are comedy shows. Americans and comedians understand this immediately. In the event that you aren't an American or a comedian, and in case I might one day call you, here are a couple of guidelines. But please don't take it too seriously. I value the guests almost as much as I do my job.

1. If you want to wing it, go to Speaker's Corner. No matter how relaxed things look, winging it does not exist in television. There will be a pre-interview. It would be nice if you had something to talk about, a reason for being in the chair other than your obvious brilliance and good looks. An anecdote or two is always good. This rule applies equally to friends of the host, people who have successfully appeared on the show before, and people who've met the host at the mall.

2. Do not answer questions with a simple yes or no more than twice. It's called shutting down the host, and if you do that, the equivalent will happen to you in the green room after the show.

3. Unless you are a genius, big-city smarty-pants who wants to be contrary. There are only three or four people in the country with this skill, and most of them are dead or in the Senate or both. Remember that you have only five minutes on one show. The host comes back night after night. The audience tunes in because they like him. So don't act snotty or try to show how smart you are. That's what my staff is for.

4. In the event that I make a mistake you have two choices. Ignore it and keep going or correct me with gentle good humour. I'm trying to make you look good. Play nice and try to do the same for me.

5. Ladies, if you wear a short skirt, a practice almost all producers and talk show hosts encourage, then please cross those legs away from the desk. Otherwise, the home audience and the producers get caught in some kind of idiotic trance, the TV version of the Bermuda triangle.

6. If the person who books you asks you not to do something, don't do it unless you are assured of being hilariously, eye-wipingly funny or you own a percentage of the network.

7. If you've gotten dressed, gone down to the studio, got your make-up on, and are about to go on stage when someone tells you that the show is long or heavy (i.e., there is no time), do not throw a hissy fit.

Show business is exactly that. Big stars take precedent over small stars. Good monologues go long. And people have to be rescheduled. It's not personal; it's just a pain in the ass for all of us.

8. If you are in a drama/melodrama/movie of the week/ television series, please pick a light, possibly comedic, moment for a clip. There is something incongruous about a rape victim and a jokey bandleader in the same five minutes.

9. Common sense suggestions: Do not get drunk, do not smoke pot in conspicuous places, do not call me a jerk-off during commercials (unless you're incredibly cute), do not break things in the green room when the canteloupe is gone, do not confuse on-screen flirtation with off-screen romance, and finally, do not scratch, chew gum, or pick your teeth on camera. I know it's hard when the host is rubbing his nose like crazy, but try. I was once pulled out of a meeting to see a slo-mo replay of a star cleaning his ears and wiping it on his sleeve. It wasn't pretty. But it was on national television.

10. The host is under no obligation to obey any of these rules. Neither are you.

Hey, Mike: Why don't you have any Canadian movie stars on your show? And what's your favourite Canadian movie?

WARD D., SALTSPRING ISLAND, B.C.

I love movies, always have. It's one of the reasons I love Toronto. They're movie-mad here. Even the homeless people have opinions about Atom Egoyan. (Sorry I didn't mention you, David Cronenberg. Eat your heart out — actually that was the plot of one of your movies, wasn't it?) Toronto is probably the only place in the world where people would line up to see the director's cut of *Caddyshack*. But I don't have any Canadian movie stars on the show for the simple reason that there are no Canadian movie stars. If we could find them, we would have them on. Canadian movie stars are actually called actors or, more specifically, waiters. As one of my producers says, there's something very strange and un-star-like about seeing a Canadian actor in a movie one day and avoiding him on the Queen Street streetcar the next. The great comedian Glen Foster says that Canadian show business is equivalent to the witness protection program (a great place to hide out). The fact is, all movie stars are American movie stars. Even if they start out Canadian, like Jim Carrey, they end up as American as Mickey Mouse and scud missiles.

What's my favourite Canadian movie? Recently I liked *Jerry & Tom*, but I've liked a lot of homegrown movies. I liked *Jesus of Montreal*. Jesus of Brampton, on the other hand, I never cared for. In fact, if you see Jesus of

Brampton, tell him I'm looking for him. He owes me money. Big time.

Hey, Mike: I notice you're going bald. Would you ever get a hair transplant like John Gallagher or Mel Lastman?

DAN P., ETOBICOKE, ONTARIO

I'll tell you, when you start to lose your hair, your relationship with everyone on the planet changes. Say, for example, that Joe Blow says hi to me. It goes like this:

Joe Blow:	*Hey, you're Mike Bullard.*
Mike:	*Hi, how you doing?*
Joe Blow:	*Pretty good. You?*
Mike:	*Fine.*
Joe Blow:	*Congratulations on the gig.*
Mike:	*Thanks a lot.*
Joe Blow:	*You take care now.*
Mike:	*Okay, see ya later.*

When you start to lose your hair, that goes something like this:

Joe Blow:	*Hey, you're Mike Bullard.*
Mike:	*Hi, how you doing?*
	(This guy's losing his hair.)
Joe Blow:	*Pretty good. You?*
Mike:	*Fine.* *(I think I've got more hair than he does.)*
Joe Blow:	*Congratulations on the gig.*

Mike:	*Thanks a lot.* (Yeah, he is really losing his hair.)
Joe Blow:	*You take care now.*
Mike:	*Okay, see ya later.* (What a baldie!)

Hey, Mike: Will you ever put out inspirational tapes like Anthony Robbins?

RICK B., MONCTON, N.B.

No. All I can provide is the following list of well-known people who prospered despite pronounced speech impediments:

1. Ed Begley, Jr. (*St. Elsewhere*)

2. Adam Arkin (*Chicago Hope*)

3. Mel Tillis (Country music star)

4. Tom Brokaw (*NBC Nightly News)*

5. Bruce Springsteen ("Born in the U.S.A.")

6. Bryan Murray (Florida Panthers GM)

7. Bob Novak (*Crossfire*)

8. Stone Phillips (*Dateline NBC*)

9. Barbara Walters (*20/20*)

10. Wallace Shawn (*The Princess Bride*)

Hey, Mike: really enjoying your show. I've decided to come see the show in person on December 14th, and as the voice-over at the end of each show indicates, guests of your show get to stay at the "Holiday Inn on Bay Street." So, I'm wondering ... what time do I check in? Do I just tell the people at the front desk that I'm one of your guests? Will there be a mini-bar in my room? Will you (or maybe Orin) be picking me up at a certain time to get to the studio? Hope to hear from you soon.

BYE FOR NOW, TIM C.

What the voice-over doesn't mention is that our guests stay at the Holiday Inn at their own expense. A Canadian talk show can only do so much.

People don't realize just how skeletal our resources are compared with American competitors. It's simple economies of scale: They have ten times our population, and therefore ten times our budget. Actually, eleven times when you consider that they access Canada as well. This puts us at a disadvantage in so many ways.

For example, a modestly funny on-the-street piece on Letterman can be dramatically improved just by running a catchy hit song underneath it. It makes a huge difference, which is why you never see a preview for a comedy movie without a popular song like "99 Red Balloons." Never.

We can't afford the thousands of dollars in rights fees, so we have to settle for Tony Padalino playing something generic on the piano. When people say our pieces drag a little compared with Letterman's, this is why. And that's just one of a thousand things.

I know that our low budget shouldn't be a concern of the audience. If I see a cheap-looking movie, I don't necessarily forgive it just because it's Canadian. In fact, I get mad because I know my tax dollars paid for the introspective piece of crap. But the next time you're wondering, "Why are they doing Canadian Way vs. American Way for the five zillionth time, instead of a slick movie parody or the Dancing Eaglesons?" you'll have the answer.

Here are some of the staffing differences between us, Conan, Letterman, and Leno:

	OPEN MIKE	CONAN	LETTERMAN	LENO
Writers	3	12	15	15
Talent bookers	3	6	8	10
Production assistants	2	6	8	8
New episodes per week	5	4	5	5

Hey, Mike: I LOVE YOU I LOVE YOU I LOVE I LOVE YOU, ETC.

ANDREA

We had three of the world's top etymologists study and restudy this e-mail. I've also put in quite a few weeks reading it — once before bed, right when I wake up, and seven or eight times throughout the day — and it's just not clear. I'll keep working on it.

HEY, MIKE, I THINK YOU HAVE THE BEST LATE NIGHT TALK SHOW ON TELEVISION. THIS MAY BE A BIASED OPINION CONSIDERING THE FACT THAT YOUR LIKE THE ONLY CANADIAN LATE NIGHT TALK SHOW HOST (I MAY BE WRONG). YOUR FORMAT IS BETTER YOU KEEP YOUR GUESTS AS OPPOSED TO SENDING THEM OFF AFTER TWO MINUTES. I LOVE THE WAY YOU MOCK THE AUDIENCE I'D LIKE TO SEE YOUR SHOW LIVE AND SIT IN THE FRONT ROW SO YOU CAN MAKE ME A PUBLIC SPECTACLE. GUESS I NEED MORE ATTENTION. A GOOD STEP WOULD BE TO TAKE A WALK INSTEAD OF SITTING IN FRONT OF A COMPUTER.

JOE C.

I think I can take care of the public spectacle issue right now by publishing your e-mail. I can't imagine what you're doing sitting in front of a computer, but I assume it would involve holding your company back from its true potential. Stop writing and speaking English.

Hey, Mike: I recently sent you an e-mail suggesting that you have the Arrogant Worms on the show. Well, I just received the latest Worms newsletter and it says that they will be on the show on December 14th. I don't know if it's just a coincidence or if you actually took my advice, but either way it was a great idea to have them on. The Arrogant Worms ROCK!!!!

THANX: BABIS R., VICTORIA

I sense the beginning of a lawsuit here. Babis, my lawyers have instructed me to inform you that it was our idea to have the Arrogant Worms on our show. And that if you did in fact have the same idea, it's purely coincidence. The same goes for some of your other suggestions of me doing more monologue jokes, putting bands at the end of the show, taking commercial breaks, and having more high-profile guests.

Hey, Mike: The whole "sharing" thing with the audience is funny, polite, generous, and quietly exploitative. Quintessentially Canadian, in fact. Tell that to your sponsors with their obscure, self-indulgent "typing monkeys" Canadian campaign, which I guarantee has not sold one ounce of lager to the beer-swilling pounders it is supposed to target. Beaver Lady, yeah, right. I give this a four out of ten.

THE CREATIVE DIRECTOR CAROL V.

I'd like to take a moment to describe to the readers what Carol must be like: Single, four cats, no friends.

Hey, Mike: I'm trying to watch the Tuesday night show with Hayden but the picture and sound aren't synched at all. As a result of this CTV technical problem your timing is REALLY off. Your reactions are coming before your punchlines. Please make this stop; it's disconcerting!

RICH, A FAN

Dear fan,
There's nothing wrong with your TV set and it was not a CTV technical problem. However, we share your sentiments.
From the writers of Open Mike

Hey, Mike: I am a little angry with you right now. I watch your show all the time and like your style of working the audience. I am a pastor and thought I would try it on Sunday morning. Gee ... it's harder than I thought. I ended up offending everyone and almost lost my job. Just thought you would find my misfortune funny.

w.

Funny? I'm not sure. Sad, yes. Here's the main problem. I go into the audience in an attempt to generate something funny and entertaining when I have no confidence in the written material that night. The written material you work from is generally thought to be pretty sound. My advice: Stick to it.

Hey, Mike: Love your show. Were you by any chance the "class clown" when you were growing up? Just curious.

JIM M., BRACEBRIDGE, ONTARIO

Not the class clown, the class snitch. I spent most of my time making sure the class clown was kicked out of school. In grade four, I sat next to this idiot, Paul, who was always shooting off his mouth. So, whenever he'd say something under his breath, I'd break into hysterics. The teacher would stop the class and ask me what was so funny and I'd respond, "It's Paul, he does the funniest impression of you mumbling under your breath." I can still hear her: "Paul, go to the office. Michael, come sit up here, honey."

Hey, Mike: Were you really a cop? If you were, why'd you quit?

TOM G.

Three months, Peel regional police. I cleaned up the town, then turned in my badge. As well, I don't think the police force enjoyed me goofing around on the job very much. They got a kick out of me razzing people on the job, they just didn't like me doing it with a loaded gun strapped to my hip. The police force wasn't for me anyhow. They had all this training, running, and fitness exercise. I didn't see the point. And, I found all the sergeants bossy. About a month into the job I had my colours done, and blue didn't cut it. I guess two things sum up the real reason I left the force: Jay-walker and shots fired.

Hey, Mike: What do you do before the show?

I'm ruled by superstitions and habits. People are always asking me why I rub my nose so much and why my finger is always in my ear. I can't stop it. I know what it looks like on national television to be wiping your nose every three seconds, but it's next to impossible for me to break a habit. In fact, I'm superstitious about breaking habits. In my opinion, you get hooked into a habit or two, don't mess around with them. The first habit I ever stumbled on to, and it became a life-altering, serious habit, was masturbating. I set records. I'm talking, at its peak, twenty to thirty times a day. When it first started, it freaked my parents out. See, I wasn't shy or awkward about it. I was on to a good thing, so why wouldn't I be doing it as often as possible? It didn't matter what images attracted me so long as it had the image of a woman on it. The *TV Guide*, the newspaper, a leaflet, an author's picture on the back of a book. Judy Blume was great. My mom had some of those old cookbooks with the picture of that housewife on the front cover and throughout the pages displaying various dishes. I used those for about half a year. Then, once a month, the Sears catalogue arrived. It would drive my mother crazy

when I'd ask, "Are you done with the catalogue?"
"Michael, leave those poor girls alone, they're just trying to make some money modelling clothes. Don't soil them with your demonic habits." Once, just to really put her over the edge, I picked up a family photo album and announced, "I'll be back in about fifteen minutes." I was presented with around ten of the finest skin magazines the following day. Of course, I don't do that any more. Now when I get the urge I rub my nose or stick my finger in my ear.

As far as superstitions go, I've got them all. Shoes on the bed, walking under ladders, open umbrellas in the house; I can't tolerate any of them. I can't pass anyone on the stairs. I've sat down at the top of a staircase and waited if there was a steady flow of traffic up and down. I've knocked on so much wood, I have calluses on my knuckles.

I was on a stand-up comedy tour across Canada with a couple of the show's writers the summer after the first season. We got to the airport and one of the guys said, "Wouldn't it be funny if our plane went down?" I waited six hours for the next flight. I guess 'cause I didn't think it would be funny! I've also made up a few superstitions of my own over the years that you're welcome to. Some of them are:

1. Don't stay in a room with your mom and dad for more than twenty minutes at a time.

2. Don't visit your mom and dad more than once every two months.

3. Don't take no for an answer when you're trying to get a talk show.

4. Don't get caught lying.

5. Keep a couple of best friends and keep everyone else guessing.

6. Only believe the good stuff you hear about yourself.

7. If you're tired, sleep.

8. If you're hungry, eat.

Hey, Mike: I love your talk show and I must say you and your brother seem born to be talk show hosts. I saw the New Year's show and I have to say it did seem a little competitive between you two. Was it always like that? And how did your parents handle it?????

CARLA B., BOUTILIERS POINT, N.S.

Oh, Carla, the stories I could tell you. It was hard on Mom and Dad at the beginning. I had my pretend talk show, Pat had his. Mom and Dad would take turns pretending to be Carol Channing and Don Rickles on my show, then on Pat's. This used to drive Mom nuts: "Stop watching TV! Why don't you kids go out and play with wood!"

But sure, like brothers everywhere, we could be cruel to each other. I'll never forget the time he told me to pole-vault onto the garage roof. I ran up and jumped, and he kicked the pole out from underneath me. The pole slipped out of my hands and stuck right to the roof of my mouth. I was suspended there for a moment, sort of spinning around with my feet dangling, and Pat, sweet Pat, he spun me around faster and faster and charged admission to see the Amazing Spinning Boy. Kids came from all around. "He's slowing down!" "Give him another spin!" And that's how I met my producer.

Hey, Mike: What is your greatest achievement? Is it the show?

TOM G.

The show is good, but I'd have to say my greatest achievement happened during a trip made to Whistler, B.C., in 1997. Let me start by saying, I don't ski. This, as it turns out, is a setback when you go skiing. The day started out poorly when I was getting my rented equipment on and asked some kid which was the left ski and which was the right one. I swear to God he said, "Mister, try to avoid me on the hills today."

I was with my best friend, and the producer of *Open Mike*, Al. He skis very well and assumes that because he can, everyone else in the world must be able to. Let me point out that as well as being my best friend, he's an asshole and told me nothing about how to ski other than, "Watch me for a bit and you'll get the hang of it." He said this on the chair-lift on our way up what seemed like about 1500 metres of mountain for our first run of the day. Needless to say, I didn't get off the chair-lift. I rode it all the way back down and back up again. As I approached the top a second time to a small crowd that had gathered around Al, most of them pointing and laughing, I could hear the lift operator over a speaker, "Put your skis down, plant your poles in the snow, and push off." Well, I planted my poles in the snow like he said and rode back down the chair-lift without them. What the hell does "push off" mean? I was now reapproaching the top for the third time. A larger crowd had gathered, and I wanted Al to die. My chair reached the top, where I had no intention of getting off, and suddenly it stopped. The whole chair-lift stopped. I stood up and pushed from the chair. Everyone applauded. I took my skis off and walked up to the chair-lift operator. "You could have done that the whole time?" "Yes," he said, "but it's not common practice." "It is today," I said. I put my skis back on and skied over to Al and punched him as hard as I could in the arm.

Incidentally, this wasn't my greatest achievement. This was just getting to the top of the hill. My greatest achievement was getting down the hill. Al brought me to the start of the expo run. He called it a fairly straightforward beginner run and gave me my first tips for skiing: "Keep your knees bent and your skis forward and together." Then he took off down the hill. I stood and watched a number of other people go down ahead of me for about half an hour, with the occasional jerk shooting a comment at me. "That chair-lift thing was the funniest thing I've ever seen. Thanks." Finally, I got too cold to stay there. Al had gone down and come back up about three times when I decided it was time for me to get off this hill. I pointed my skis forward and started down the hill.

For a while, I was the fastest skier on the hill. I was passing everyone who seemed to be slowing themselves down with these constant turns. Then I plowed right into one of them. My head hit one of my skis about three times before I stopped rolling. My other ski was about a hundred metres down the hill pointing forward! That was it. My skiing days were over. I picked up my ski and made my way down to the other one. I stayed there, had a cigarette, and talked to a few people to try to find out why the hell they would bother with the stupid sport. Most had been doing it since they were five or six and let me know that it takes a long time to get the hang of it, especially on a run like the expo. Again, I wanted Al to die. I got up and continued my walk down the hill, stopping every ten minutes or so for a rest and a smoke. I reached the bottom about two and a half hours later. I was in the chalet nursing some blisters when a ski patroller came up to me and said that in the nine years he had worked there, "No one has ever walked all the way down Whistler."

Well, that's something.

Hey, Mike: You're a pretty normal-looking guy, but do you get a lot more chicks and sex now that you're a TV star?

ADRIAN B.

Adrian, you don't know how long I spent wondering if you're a man or a woman. But why should that change my answer? What does that say about me as a sensitive, caring, but passionately full-blooded North American man who has his own talk show and drives a Yamaha? Listen, Adrian, the bald truth is that any old fool with a talk show can pick up women. To get women the old way, by whining and wheedling and making them feel sorry for you, now that takes a young fool. Here are some ideas that I think might help:

1. Get into a rhythm. This can take longer to learn than you think. I finally broke down and put a metronome on the floor, but that complicated things when I started breaking into "Chopsticks" in quiet moments.

2. Cleanliness. Chicks sometimes want you to talk dirty, but they don't want you to be dirty.

3. Research. You'd be surprised what you can learn in books. Handy tip: Buy your own sex books. I once lifted a book from my parents' bedroom and spent three years developing my pelvic floor without realizing I didn't have one.

4. Know your limits. If it's going on for too long and your partner's bored, cut your losses: Fake the orgasm and move on.

Hey, Mike: Does being fat and bald help you be funny? I'm thinking of getting into comedy. Should I shave my head and eat a bunch of chips before I do?

SUNIL, SASKATCHEWAN

Yes. Sunil. You. Should. Why? Because good-looking male comedians (and I'm assuming you consider your-self handsome here, Sunil, because only a good-looking crap artist like yourself would bother writing such a hurtful letter. Have you noticed that, folks? Good-looking people on the whole are less compassionate and forgiving than we regular mortals. I curse them as they've cursed me!) what was I saying? Oh, yes. Good-looking male comedians already have two strikes against them.

1. Women will be suspect of whether you are funny. Why would a handsome guy have to be funny? It's really an either/or situation.

2. Guys already have so much resentment towards you that when you walk out on stage they will not pay attention to the first couple of things you say or do.

So here's my limited professional advice to you, Sunil. The first thing you should do when you walk out on stage is make a self-deprecating comment. That's the only way anyone will respect you.

Hey, Mike: How are you with confrontation?

HENRY, CALGARY

What's your point? Good comedy comes out of confrontation. Can somebody give me better questions? You people have computers. You're supposed to be smart and moneyed and educated. Surely you can come up with some better questions than this. Old Sunil up there is starting to look like a genius compared to you people, and he wants to be a comedian!

Hey, Mike: I think you're a bully.

SALLY, MCMASTER UNIVERSITY

Succinct. To the point. Firm. I like it. But IT'S NOT A QUESTION! Let me tell you about bullies anyway. In grade eight I had to walk up the middle of the highway on my way home from school. Why? Because four jocks took me aside and told me they were going to beat me up unless I did. So I did. Then one day my old man passes me and stops the car and asks what the hell I'm doing. I told him. So he went out and beat the hell out of those guys.

Okay, so that's not really what happened, but I have to save something for the second book.

Hey, Mike: Women seem to like you. Why do you suppose that is?

DARREN, TRURO, N.S.

Well, Darren, since you've asked, I think I've redefined sexiness in the country (but I don't like to brag). I think there are fat, bald guys across this country getting gratuitous sex, and they have me to thank for it.

Hey, Mike: I love the way you handle hecklers. What's the worst heckler you ever had and how did you handle him/her?

LESTER P., SWIFT CURRENT, SASKATCHEWAN

No, I'm not afraid of hecklers any more. I welcome them. Anything to relieve the strain of coming up with material. Hell, hecklers are my material. In the beginning I was scared of them, though. Terrified. Even outside a comedy club I was scared of them. I'd be walking down the street and someone would yell, "Hey, buddy. You suck!" And I'd turn around and be so relieved that they were talking to their friend or to a starving homeless person. Yes, I was relieved because my secret would be safe for another day. But you know how I got over it? I realized that if hecklers have this need to be heard and to interrupt others, they're probably the guys who do the graffiti in public bathrooms. Like if I wasn't in the TV studio and the hecklers could get away with it, they'd be up against the wall scribbling bad drawings of female torsos. Let me just say that I have never felt compelled to deface bathroom walls with bad limericks. What is it about a bathroom that brings out the worst in people — aside from it being a bathroom? I hate it that oddballs try to dishonour the most sacred sexual acts with the worst kinds of graffiti. "Your mother sucks wieners in hell," that kind of thing. I remember one day I'd had enough and I said, "Face it, Dad — you've got a problem! Deal with it."

Hey, Mike: Who is your favourite comedian?

SALLY, LETHWAY, SASKATCHEWAN

Well, that's simple: Garry Shandling. It was 1990. I went to see him at Donald Trump's casino in Atlantic City because my brother was playing there. Well, Pat wasn't playing there. He was headlining at something called the Comedy Trough, but anyway Al and I went to see Shandling and it was the first time that I realized you could walk out into a room in front of four thousand people and spritz.

Hey, Mike: Do mice fart????

SHAG68

Okay, this is why I believe the Internet will never have the impact people say it will. The information superhighway is jammed with gems like this one, along with nude footage of Kelsey Grammar and sites like www.oddcouple2.com. If you're remotely interested in the sequel to *The Odd Couple*, are you likely to be online? Of course not — you're eighty. It's like promoting *Dawson's Creek* on AM radio — a complete waste of time.

The e-mail revolution is the most ridiculous BS since Rosie O'Donnell's supposed crush on Tom Cruise. One of my writers has a stand-up bit where he points out that if e-mail had been around for fifty years, and suddenly they introduced the telephone, people would be saying, "Oh, forget e-mail — you gotta get a phone! It's way better — you can talk to the person! Why, yes it does have applications for business...."

Some have said that the Internet will replace television as we know it by providing viewers with the opportunity to watch any show whenever they want. In fact, we gained that opportunity when they invented the VCR. That's when we all began the now-familiar routine of taping shows and never watching them. There just aren't many television shows so compelling that you would commit to setting the VCR *and* rewinding *and* viewing. It's like bumping into an old high school friend and promising to get together *and* actually calling them — it sounds practical but it's clearly not.

TV will survive and thrive the way movie theatres have. Cinemas have been on the way out for seventy-five years. Box-office revenues continue to set new records every year. Why would anyone pay $8 to see a movie in a crowded theatre when they can see it in the privacy of their home for $4? Because they like the big screen, they need to go on dates, they need to have their kid's birthday party somewhere, they need to escape from their spouse for an afternoon, they don't have air conditioning, — every reason you can imagine except for the friendly service of which the theatre chains are so proud. After three hours of watching Private Ryan's platoon get wiped out, nobody cares if the usher says goodbye.

In fact, wouldn't it be interesting if the cost of fixing the year 2000 computer problem ends up wiping out the entire amount computers have saved us since their invention? I know our show will be devastated when, on January 1, 2000, my monologue consists entirely of jokes from the year 1900. Look out President McKinley, you're about to get zinged again.

I have the solution to the Y2K problem, so I hope the people in charge of the computers at the utility companies, the airlines, the Pentagon, etc., are reading this: When the year 2000 hits, shut all the computers off. Then turn them on again. If that doesn't work, turn them off and on again. If that *still* doesn't work, then call somebody. But I'm pretty sure it'll work, because I've used a computer for a couple of years now and that's what I always do.

But to address your inquiry about whether mice fart, Shag68: QUIT WASTING MY TIME WITH INANE QUESTIONS.

Hey, Mike: Ever have erotic dreams of CBC news-women?

YOUR FRIEND AND FELLOW CANADIAN, ROB

Now we're getting somewhere. Here's my list of the hottest newswomen in Canadian TV:

1. Wendy Mesley, CBC. Such an obvious choice that she shouldn't be eligible for these lists any more, the way hockey pools didn't let you pick Gretzky when he was in his prime.

2. Dawna Friesen, CTV Newsnet. European-type sophistication. Once when I was watching her and the phone rang, I turned the sound down but felt compelled to keep watching her for an hour while I was talking on the phone. God, they repeat their stories a lot on that channel. Is any of it live?

3. Holly Doan, CTV. I thought two years of corresponding from China would make her look pretty weathered, but I swear she looks even better than when she left. Are those collective farms over there or spas?

4. Laurie Brown, CBC. She didn't mean much to me until I met her in person. Everyone should have the chance to meet her in person.

5. Martine, the Weather Network. She's an eight out of ten — nine with the Humidex. If you ever meet her in a bar, you have my permission to use that line.

6. Lisa Laflamme, CTV Newsnet. Her stripper name doesn't belong in TV news, but to be honest, it started the thought process that led to her inclusion on this list. She always sounds like she has a cold, but I don't think it's possible to have a cold all the time. I guess she was sick the day News1 taped its updates for the year.

7. Laine Fraser, CTV Newsnet. She works for the Toronto affiliate CFTO, but fills in occasionally on Newsnet. I'd put her in the top three if she had a higher national profile. She's the only one with the potential to challenge Wendy Mesley, but does she have the ambition?

8. Hana Gartner, CBC. There's no substitute for experience.

9. Rebecca Rankin, Muchmusic. I had to include someone from ChumCity or Moses Znaimer would ban his people from appearing on my show.

10. Valerie Pringle, CTV. Admit it — you've all thought about it.

Now, in the interests of equality, I had the women at *Open Mike* and Doubleday come up with their list of the ten hottest newsmen in Canadian TV.

1. Lloyd Robertson

2. Lloyd Robertson

3. Lloyd Robertson

4. Lloyd Robertson

5. Lloyd Robertson

6. Lloyd Robertson

7. Lloyd Robertson

8. Lloyd Robertson

9. Lloyd Robertson

10. Lloyd Robertson

Hey, I notice you and Orin hit fists at the beginning of every show. Why?

JACKEL

To keep it real, you idiot.

Actually, it's the current "I'm too cool for a regular handshake" move that traces its roots back to the original "gimme five" hand slap. Along the way came the high-five, that arm-wrestling-style handshake, the fist-on-top-of-fist, and other variations designed to show the world that, no matter how hard it tries, it'll never be able to keep up with *you*. That you don't take your cues from the Man, you take them directly from the street. That you have no interest in playing in the other reindeer's games.

Even as I write this, Jackel, the cool establishment is on high alert because shows like mine are popularizing the fist-hit among cable-subscribing computer nerds like you. A multinational subcommittee co-chaired by Damon Wayans and YTV's PJ Phil is currently brainstorming on a new handshake, to be unveiled in time for Christmas 1999.

Also on its last legs is that "raise the roof" gesture that was reasonably cool on *Showtime at the Apollo*, less cool on *Vibe*, and completely unacceptable on the *Donny & Marie Show*.

Hey, Mike: How long will it be before Doug Flutie comes to the show and kicks your butt?

SINCERELY, GIL R., OTTAWA

My sports-minded writers tell me Flutie isn't a butt-kicker, he's a scrambler. He dodges defensive linemen, but worst of all, ran away from his talk show commitment. And I've decided to take it personally.

For anyone wondering what all this is about, the e-mail is referring to our constant jokes about Doug Flutie in the monologue. I'm not sure we've ever explained this on the air, but the whole thing goes back to December 19, 1997. I remember it like it was only yesterday....

It was our last show before Christmas, scheduled to feature then-Argo Doug Flutie. We were in a festive mood because our office Christmas party was right after the show, to be followed by a long-awaited vacation. But the giddiness ground to a halt when we found out three hours before showtime that Flutie wasn't coming. Suddenly, we faced the prospect of going into the Christmas break with a show featuring twelve minutes of dead air.

After failing to line up a replacement guest, we put head writer Lawrence Morgenstern in a Santa Claus suit and took live phone calls from children. And you know what? It was so heart-warming and uplifting that we decided to do it on the show next year too.

Although the Santa segment did work beautifully, I never really got over my co-workers' sad little faces at the Christmas party when they found out Flutie wasn't coming. It's the TV equivalent of a lump of coal.

There was much talk of Flutie taking the Buffalo Bills to the Super Bowl in 1999, but the Bills crashed and burned before that. Imagine how heartbroken they would have been if they had made it all the way to the Super Bowl, and then their quarterback hadn't felt like showing up for the big game. Come to think of it, Bills fans are probably used to heartbreak.

And just in case anyone who knows Flutie reads this book, I want you to know that I read the whole Flutie book in preparation for his interview. And just in case Doug Flutie ever does come on my show he better have read this book.

Don't you think that reading viewers' e-mail on Open Mike is kind of familiar? Not that I am saying that is bad thing, it's just that David Letterman does the same on his show.

MICHAEL

Michael, don't you think your first name is kind of familiar? It's been done.

I'm not suggesting it's okay to steal ideas, but not everything is an idea you can copyright. My name is Mike, and the host of the *Mike Douglas Show* was named Mike. Is that stealing? Letterman has a desk, just like Johnny Carson did. Is that stealing? Of course not. Johnny Carson's "Carnak" routine was basically the same as Steve Allen's "Answer Man." Does that make Johnny a thief? Sure, and you could always tell that Steve Allen had a big problem with it.

Our show has never stolen a comedic idea, unlike your beloved Letterman, whose "suit of Alka Seltzer" was a direct rip-off of Steve Allen's "suit of tea bags." Since Letterman later acknowledged he was stealing, Steve Allen still speaks well of him.

Answering mail is not a comedic idea any more than sending mail is. It's the *jokes* you make while answering the mail that need to be original. If I can't think of an original joke, I won't resort to stealing — I'll just say something hateful instead. I've got to be true to myself.

ON HATING TORONTO

Whenever I go on tour around the country people tell me that they hate Toronto. And then they tell me why. And usually when they tell me, they have a really silly grin on their face, which in some way is meant to indicate how pleased they are that they have finally found a real Torontonian to vent at. What surprises me about these people is that they think I have not heard these arguments before. In some strange way, they think they are the first person to have the courage to hate Toronto. So, to set the record straight, let me make this clear: Hating Toronto is as Canadian as hockey. We invented it. Everybody hates Toronto. And people from Toronto have all heard all of the reasons why you hate Toronto. In fact, telling Torontonians that you hate Toronto only reinforces their natural superiority complex, because you are boring them.

In an effort for us all to get along, I thought that, once and for all, I'd not only list the most common complaints of the rest of the country but also answer them with the best big-city, stuck-up-bastard point of view that I can muster.

Rest of Canada: Torontonians think the country revolves around them.

Toronto: Why are you always talking about us if you are so disinterested?

Rest of Canada: Torontonians buy up choice rural properties and then complain that there is no cappuccino.

Toronto: Cappuccino went out sometime around 1995. Keep up. Now we complain that there are no organic vegetables and fresh herbs in the middle of pastoral Canada.

Rest of Canada: Torontonians do not care about the rest of the country.

Toronto: Have you heard of the phrase "transfer payment"?

Rest of Canada: Torontonians only care about money.

Toronto: (See above.) We also care about keeping up with the Joneses, beating Montreal in everything from population to art exhibits, and maintaining hundreds of neighbourhood street festivals and parades that have no meaning to the rest of the population aside from screwing up traffic.

Rest of Canada: There are too many cars in Toronto.

Toronto: Yes, but our street festivals are colourful.

Rest of Canada: Toronto sucks compared to New York.

Toronto: If you take this a step further and say that Canada sucks compared to the United States, the same people who say Toronto sucks will report you for treason. "Oh no," they'll protest with a nationalistic gleam in their eyes. "There is less crime and less racism in Canada."

Then they'll drag out universal health care. So yes, let us agree, New York is a way more exciting place than Toronto. To visit. Just try finding an apartment there (and, no, I don't mean in Brooklyn).

Rest of Canada: Canadian media are saturated with stories about Toronto because the media people all live in Toronto and they are all navel-gazing snivellers.

Toronto: Canadian media are saturated with stories about Toronto because the media people all live in Toronto and they are all navel-gazing snivellers. But where did they come from? Kick the CBC Broadcast Centre and people from small towns who migrated to the city will scramble out like rats. So blame your sons and daughters and neighbours who left. They are the Toronto media. Except for Valerie Pringle. She's from Rosedale.

Rest of Canada: East Coast: Torontonians are too conservative. West Coast: Torontonians are too liberal.

Toronto: It's hard being the middle child.

Rest of Canada: Toronto is too fast. Torontonians are too impatient and rude.

Toronto: Okay, so there are big highways and people drive over the speed limit. And, yes, we get used to trying to cram as much as we can into a day, but that's because we're all sitting in traffic for two hours every day.

Rest of Canada: Torontonians are stuck-up, snobby bastards.

Toronto: Okay, so the character of Toronto is still dominated by Type-A Victorians who were obsessed with getting enough going into this crazy country that the Brits wouldn't let the Americans invade. Can you blame them? I mean, really, what was going on in this country until recently? Plus, the rest of the country's got its boorish side, too. Vancouverites act like they invented the idea of mountains and ocean. And on the East Coast everybody is so friendly and noncompetitive that ambition is considered rude. Quebec is so snobby they've given up even talking to the rest of Canada. And the prairies, well, I have no complaints about anyone from Winnipeg to Alberta. They managed to stay friendly and invent health care. Plus, they don't drag you into a field every time you visit.

So the next time your friends or family come home from Toronto for Christmas, please don't regale them with tales of how you hate Toronto. We don't mind if you hate us, just don't tell us about it.

ON THOSE OTHER CITIES: MONTREAL AND VANCOUVER

While I do make fun of Quebec a lot on the show, I have to say that I love Montreal. But even though I love it, I know that I could never live there. Same with Vancouver. I am simply too cranky to live there. How Montrealers can drink so much coffee and still seem relaxed is a mystery to me. Maybe it's the smoking. At least in Vancouver they get a bit rangy from all that Starbucks.

Hey, Mike: You seem to slag Easterners a lot on your show. Why? What's up with that? Have you ever even been to God's Country?

A.P., PARKWOOD, NOVA SCOTIA

First of all, I slag everybody. That's my job. Second, never ever use the phrase "what's up with that?" Finally, yes, of course I've been to God's Country, and I cherish the memory of each magical boyhood visit. Every summer we'd visit my distant family back east or out east or way down east or whatever the hell you Maritimers call it.

The hub of my mother's world used to be P.E.I., and so each August we'd visit Auntie Grace and Uncle Buddy-in-the-Wheelchair for some down-home hospitality. Now Buddy-in-the-Wheelchair and Grace, they didn't have the most luxurious home in the world — think slanted house, cracked furnace, half-eaten cat food hardening in chipped cereal bowls — so as soon as we'd arrive fresh from the eighty-seven-hour ferry ride from the mainland, Uncle Buddy-in-the-Wheelchair would make us drive him out to his cottage — which he called a cabin, which was actually a shack. Buddy had emphysema back then, of course, and was down to only six packs of Cameo menthols a day, but he couldn't quite wheel himself over the rocks and moss so each of his eight kids would take a turn pushing the rickety old wheelchair.

Buddy and Grace had four boys and four girls and you'd think they'd be happy with the split, but Buddy's mind was a strange place. (Quick example: When I hit my thumb with a hammer I immediately scream, "Ahh!" When Buddy hit his thumb with a hammer he used to wait five seconds and then say, "*Faaa* me gently" very slowly.) Anyway, out East if they get a girl and want a son, they just put an "a" on the end of a boy's name, like Roberta or Paula or Shawna. So the four daughters Buddy had were, I'm not kidding now, Alexa, Simona, Kevina, and, my favourite, Arnolda. (Arnolda? I mean, I'd rather be called Flotilla or Placenta — not a bad name, Placenta.)

Inevitably the girls would tire out, and I would be enlisted to push our hacking, swearing uncle down the path to his shack. If we didn't spill him out of the chair, his inevitable temper tantrum would be put off till later, so he'd tour us around the place. He was on Worker's Comp at the time and spent his leisure hours inventing an electric canoe, a timesaving device he had been tinkering with since the days when Newfoundland was a British colony. After a few hours of cheery small talk, Uncle Buddy-in-the-Wheelchair might see one of his four neighbours, or listen to the CBC, or overhear my mother talking to someone on the phone. Then his mood would darken, and it wasn't long before he was glaring at you, talking about the "goddamn Knights of Columbus," or the Masons and daring people to take a swing at him. And people wonder where I got my charming disposition.

It was a special, magical time, and one that has been burned into my memory like a brand. My mother used to describe Buddy as "disgruntled." "Mom," I used to say, "has he ever been gruntled?" Actually, I don't know if I've ever been gruntled. Just once, if I had my druthers, I'd like to be gruntled. I'd like all four of our Maritime provinces to be gruntled. Wait. One of my producers just threw a stapler at me. Apparently Newfoundland's an "Atlantic" province, not a "Maritime" one. Ah, Maritimers: the Canadian's Canadian.

Hey, Mike: Is it true you hate hockey? Did you get disillusioned as a kid?

HANK B., WHITBY, ONTARIO

I don't know if I exactly hate hockey, Hank, I just don't know anything about it. I'm reminded of what the great Canadian poet Al Purdy once said about hockey: "And how do the players feel about it, this combination of ballet and murder?" That's getting at the truth of it, but then again I've never read Al Purdy, so I don't know anything about him either. Hockey, hockey, hockey. The goddamned stuff is everywhere. What is it about this great northern land that breeds hockey players? Russia produces their fair share of hockey geniuses, too, like Federov and Bure and Tretiak. I'm reminded of what the great Russian novelist Dostoyevsky once said about Russia: "My name's Raskalnikov, I'm a student." But then again I've never read Dostoyevsky, so I don't know what the hell that line means. In fact, I didn't even write it. My editor made me put it in. Basically, as a kid hockey meant not getting to watch what I wanted to watch on Saturday nights or getting grounded for pouring Pepsi on my brother's Esso Power Players collection. Of course, over the years I've mellowed and we've had Eddie Shack, Howie Meeker, Tie Domi, and Tiger Williams on the show, not to mention countless sports journalists flogging their non-fiction books about hockey, their novels about hockey, their sonnets about hockey. I've got enough hockey books in the basement to keep my Uncle Buddy-in-the-Wheelchair's wood stove going for a month of Sundays. Apparently it's the only kind of book that sells in this country, the only thing that men will read. Now if only Carol Shields wrote about hockey, then she'd really have a best seller. But then again I've never read Carol Shields, and in fact I don't even know who she is. Is that a real name? My wife made me put her in.

Hey, Mike: You have a lot of authors on the show. Do you actually read all their books? Which ones are your favourites and which are your favourite books?

MRS. KELLY C.

Of course I read. Didn't you just see the previous entry? My favourite authors are Al Purdy, Dostoyevsky, Carol Shields, and Howie Meeker.

Hey, Mike: You seemed to get along pretty well with that gay sex columnist Dan Savage guy. Are you gay or what?

BRUCE B.

Am I gay? Well, when my cousins moved up here from P.E.I. they lived the next street over from us in Mississauga. One of the years that my parents abandoned me, I had to live with Uncle Buddy-in-the-Wheelchair and Auntie Grace, and that was the year when four of their eight kids came out of the closet. As kids, my brothers and I always knew our cousins were different but we didn't know they were gay; we just thought they were sophisticated. I remember the day Freddy and Earl came out. I was down with Earl in the rec room trying to get his mother's dress zipped up on him. Freddy came in. He was breathless.

"Earl," he said. "I just told Mom and Dad."

"Really?" said Earl. "What'd they say?"

"Well, I think they were okay with it."

"Wow. That's excellent." (This was back in the seventies when people said "excellent.")

So Earl went to talk to his parents and I followed to spy on them.

"Mom, Dad?" said Earl.

"Yes, Earl?" said Auntie Grace.

"Well, I wanted to say ... I'm gay, just like Freddy. I'm a homosexual."

"You're a *what*?" said Uncle Buddy-in-the-Wheelchair, looking up for the first time from the TV listings. "What the hell are you talking about?"

"Earl," said Auntie Grace. "Freddy just said he was confused about his sexuality."

"Oh," said Earl. "That's what I meant. I'm confused. Like Freddy. Uh, what's for supper? Pork chops? My favourite. See ya!" And he ran out, leaving me alone in the hallway. Uncle Buddy threw the telecaster on the floor and looked at me. "Flamers, Michael," he said to me. "I'm surrounded. Where do you sit on this?" It was one of the only times in my life that I didn't have a snappy comeback.

That was a long while ago now, back before it was trendy to be gay. Because for a while there, everybody was gay. Remember those days? And sure, I felt left out. I mean, I tried. God knows I tried. I can't tell you the number of nights I'd tag along with my cousins to the bars, dressing up in the T-shirts and the leather pants and the cap and the rubber, zippered cowl. But it just didn't work. No matter how hard I tried, I didn't fit in. It was like trying to stick a square peg in a round hole. It just wasn't happening. So no, Bruce, I'm not gay. (Your name's Bruce and you're asking me if I'm gay?) I'm not even very sophisticated. But I hope to be. That's my goal. Because you've got to have goals.

Hey, Mike: I don't have cable and your show is on CTV too late. What should I do?

P.J.O.

Get cable.

My Childhood in Canada	What Might Have Been in America
Mike Bullard is a fat kid who can't skate.	Mike Bullard is a really fat kid who can't skate.
Mike Bullard's mother encourages him to drink his milk so he grows up big and strong.	Mike Bullard becomes the first abducted child whose head shot doesn't fit on to the milk carton.
A young Mike Bullard hones his comedy on the open stage.	A young Mike Bullard is denied stage time due to a glut of stubbly drifters with no material.
Mike Bullard gets work as a comic despite having very few prepared lines.	Mike Bullard gets work with the prepared line, "Hi, welcome to Wal-Mart."
A young Mike Bullard's manliness is questioned because he doesn't drink beer.	A young Mike Bullard's manliness is questioned for dodging a different kind of draft.
Mike Bullard is constantly nagged about why he doesn't try to make it in America.	Ditto.
Mike Bullard is eventually welcomed among the show-biz elite.	Mike Bullard is eventually sold a firearm despite disturbing emotional and mental traits.

Hey, Mike: I know you're busy with the show, but do you think you could find time to run for Prime Minister? The health care system needs fixing, and you're the one to do it. Think of the children.
P.S.: You might want to use different speech-writers than the ones you employ now! They bite!

JT, BRANDON, MANITOBA

Believe me, JT, my number-one priority has always been the children. I believe we must invest in our children, because they represent the future. Just like we can neglect our seniors, because they represent the past.

My solution to the overcrowding in hospital waiting rooms is simple: I will send people walking through every half hour to make the following announcement: "If you are here because of a skateboarding injury, get lost!" The one thing the fathers of socialized medicine didn't consider was that thousands of young people would decide to jump off a curb on a rolling piece of plywood. I think we can all agree that the price of stupidity in our society should be a broken tailbone.

Another thing I'll do to help unclog the health care system is continue smoking. The dirty little secret behind the legalization of smoking is that society saves billions of dollars when people like me die before claiming pension benefits. The cost of cancer treatments in my fifties and sixties is offset by the cost of non-smokers' everything else treatments in their eighties and nineties.

I have lots of opinions on politics, but I generally keep them to myself in order to remain as popular as possible.

Just like Jean Chrétien. But as a courtesy to those of you who bought this book hoping for the answers to society's ills, here are some of the ways I'll make things better:

Legalizing All Consensual Acts

Laws against drugs, prostitution, and ticket-scalping are unenforceable. They also cost us all a lot of money, because drug dealers, hookers, and scalpers don't pay taxes. We also spend money fruitlessly by paying police to chase these people around. Whether or not you believe in drug use, it can be stopped only on the demand side. Put a drug dealer in prison and his clients will find somebody else. But if drug education programs make people quit, that puts dealers out of business, while leaving our prison cells free for the people who really belong there: jaywalkers.

Let's also remember that innocent people are maimed and killed when drug addicts seek money to pay for their fixes. The price of illicit drugs is so high because they have to be smuggled into the country at great risk to the smuggler. If crack was legal, it could be mass-produced by companies like Molson for pennies a vial. And who wouldn't want to see the TV commercials for Molson Crack? If you think the beer drinkers are having fun ...

My basic point, and who could argue, is that we should take the drug profits out of the hands of criminals and put them into the hands of governments and private investors, while also eliminating violent drug-related attacks against innocent people. Can you believe we haven't done this all along? Am I the only sane person in the universe? If so, then I should at least be the prime minister.

The Party's Over for Quebec

It's pretty clear that most of us want Quebec to stay, but as long as we keep begging and bribing them, the spectre of separation will never go away because they enjoy our grovelling too much. All we have to do to make this issue disappear is lay it on the line: We'd like you to stay under the current rules, or else you can go and lose all privileges of trade and citizenship. Frankly, the argument that Quebecers are treated as second-class citizens in Canada is totally undermined by the fact that the prime minister's office has been occupied by a Quebecer for twenty-eight out of the last thirty years.

If Quebec leaves, we then wait for the Montreal referendum. When they inevitably vote to rejoin Canada but are refused by Lucien Bouchard, we send our troops in there and take back what is rightfully ours. That's right, we start killing each other. Then the survivors can spend the next twenty years re-establishing water and power lines. By the way, if you said "Yeah!" after reading the part about sending our troops into Quebec, please don't ever breed.

We have to just let Quebec go, taking with them land that really doesn't belong to them and leaving behind debts that do, and console ourselves with the knowledge that Lucien Bouchard and his ilk will go straight to hell for breaking up one of the few peaceful countries on the globe in order to further their personal ambitions.

Abolish the Senate

What on earth is it for? And why should anyone be paid for work if they don't show up? Oh, yeah — my monologue! Forget this part.

More Public Transit in the Big Cities

It's so obvious. As the air becomes less and less breatheable, everyone should be taking trains and buses. Also, a bus can transport fifty people while taking up the road space of about two cars. In other words, once we get all those cars off the road, I'll be able to drive to work with virtually no traffic in my way. It's not an urgent issue, though, because right now I get from my roof to the Masonic Temple in about five minutes courtesy of the CTV News helicopter. That Dini Petty is some pilot!

Maximum Driving Age

Thanks to an aging society, we've got human time bombs all over the roads. As they start to have more and more heart attacks at the wheel, it's going to become obvious that we can't have eighty-year-olds driving cars. Some people, mostly representatives of the auto glass industry, will tell you that some eighty-year-olds can drive and that they can be tested to make sure they have all the necessary skills. I'll tell you that some twelve-year-olds could probably drive, too, but we don't let them because it's an unnecessary risk. Whether or not I become prime minister, the maximum driving age will become a hot topic within fifteen years.

Study Philosophy on Your Own Dime

To free up money for students of medicine, engineering, and other stuff that really matters, my government would no longer subsidize university classes in the areas of philosophy, Latin, or Greek mythology. Can you think of any valued personal possession that was made possible in any way by a graduate of these disciplines? Face it, knowing anything about any of the aforementioned subjects only leads to misery. Have you ever met a philosopher? Tragic.

Standardized Testing

All elementary school students would be required to read this book and pass a standardized test on its content.

Absolutely No Subsidies for Pro Sports

Olympic Stadium and SkyDome are two great examples of a staggering waste of public money in the name of pro sports. Now the federal government appears to be on the verge of creating huge subsidies for the likes of the Montreal Canadiens and the Calgary Flames, in response to the threat that they'll pack up and leave. Who really believes the Montreal Canadiens will leave that city? Even I, who know nothing about hockey, can see that. The Canadiens' market is all of Quebec, a region with ten million raving hockey fans who watch the games and buy the merchandise. Where would they go? Houston has a few million people, out of which a few hundred thousand might actually care about hockey.

This is one of the most ridiculous bluffs in the history of the world.

As for the Calgary Flames, did it ever occur to anyone that some cities just aren't big enough to support a big-league sports team? The job creation argument is total BS. Who wants our tax dollars supporting millionaire athlete jobs and minimum-wage usher jobs? The whole notion that domes and sports franchises generate economic benefits has never really been substantiated. Most of the tickets are bought by locals who would've spent the money in the community anyway. And don't tell me that hockey is too vital to cities like Calgary and Edmonton to let these teams leave, because there were no NHL teams there until 1979 and the game flourished at the grass roots level anyway.

Besides, what's the point of giving $5 million to Theoren Fleury, if it leaves you with no money to build more rinks to develop more Theoren Fleurys.

The Death Penalty

Couldn't we just use it now and again? Please, Mom? At a time when we don't have enough radiation machines for cancer patients, it seems ridiculous that we're paying to feed Paul Bernardo three times a day. We can call it "The Bernardo Law," meaning that it applies only to purely evil murderers whose guilt is overwhelmingly proven. Of course, this could hurt my ratings on the Comedy Network, because I'll bet the government provides Paul Bernardo and Clifford Olsen with the full cable package.

Maximum Wages

It makes no sense that corporate executives make
million-dollar salaries while the people at the bottom get
$6 an hour. The only reason executives get that kind of
money is that their salaries are determined by other
executives, who want to set a high precedent for when
their own salaries are reviewed. That's not capitalism. The
only people who should make millions are people who
bear risks, such as entrepreneurs and investors. There
also should be allowances for athletes and entertainers,
or anyone else who's exposed directly to a business's end
user. I don't think you can establish that anyone chose to
bank with the CIBC because of anything done by CEO
Al Flood, so why should he be taking home $2 million?
It actually shows what a bad CEO he is, because that
kind of salary can only hurt the morale of the workers
at the bottom.

[Ed: Mike, I feel I have to point out that your interns
are unpaid. Mike: Oops! Disregard that last bit.]

Fingerprint All Citizens

Don't give me that Big Brother crap. Big Brother's already
watching everybody; he's been doing it for fifteen years.
But Big Brother is still having a hard time keeping a few
welfare recipients from collecting over and over because
there's no quick way of identifying claimants. Fingerprinting is the answer, and since I read that welfare
recipients think fingerprinting them would create an
unwanted stigma, I'll fingerprint everybody. This will also
expedite my interaction with the audience at the show:

Instead of asking people who they are and where they're from, I'll just scan their fingertips. When the data appear on my monitor, I'll be able to get right to the hilarious bits instead of waiting all night for intelligible answers like I do now.

Hey, Mike: Like what gives with you and your writers always being so critical of Premier Mike Harris of Ontario? I'd just like to take a time out to say what a great job I think Premier Harris is doing on behalf of the Ontario Conservative party and the people of Ontario. Like, let's hear it for someone who has really got this place moving forward again. We appreciate it. And I'd also like to address the fact that some of you have come down really hard on him because he hasn't read every book in the world. I think that's disgusting. In my school they made us read all of these books that had nothing to do with anything, so I don't think Harris should be wasting his time with books when he has a job running this country. And for all those people out there who want people to read every book in the world, I would just say, Get a Life.

I'm not even going to touch this one.

SIGNS YOU MIGHT BE A CANADIAN

You may think having a birth certificate that says you were born in Canada proves you're a Canadian. But what if you lose it? What if you're struck on the head by a falling chunk of Olympic Stadium, and when you wake up, you don't know who you are? Or what if you've moved to the United States and forgotten your roots? All of this could happen to you. So, to be safe, keep a copy of this list in your back pocket at all times.

1. You don't feel the urge to purchase maple syrup at the airport.

2. When in Niagara Falls, you scoff at how pathetic the American falls are compared to the Canadian ones.

3. You've plugged a car in overnight.

4. You're not easily impressed by British accents.

5. You're easily impressed by British accents.

6. You assume the channel you're watching the Super Bowl on probably isn't showing the really good commercials.

7. You own a copy of the Bob and Doug record on CD, but refuse to admit to anyone that you've ever said "eh" in your life.

8. You fly into a rage in a Los Angeles 7-Eleven because they don't sell Crispy Crunch.

9. You would feel safe leaving your children alone with a grown man in a leotard playing a flute to a rooster.

10. You've defended your property from trespassers with a lacrosse stick because you don't own a gun.

11. When a weather reporter on American television blames the cold weather on a Canadian front, you giggle like you had something to do with it.

12. You don't have to call it "ice" hockey.

13. To you the term "roughrider" doesn't imply gay sex.

14. You catch yourself humming the "Log Driver's Waltz."

15. You know the names of every major brand of breakfast cereal and Vachon cake in both English and French.

16. You can remember when Alanis Morissette was a dance act.

17. You've never been in a crowd of 80,000 to watch a single high-school football game.

18. You don't assume that RCMP officers have beautiful singing voices.

19. You don't think that Saskatchewan is a hoax pulled off by a guy in a gorilla suit.

20. You've been forced to watch a vignette on the inventors of the snowmobile before you watch a feature film.

21. Your parents live in Florida.

22. You can't name five Canadian prime ministers, but you know the first name of everyone related to Wayne Gretzky.

23. You're reading this list to kill time in a hospital emergency room.

24. You have a bumper sticker on your car that protests the GST, but when you bought it you paid the goddamn tax.

25. You've made a casserole with more than five different kinds of cheese.

26. You've desperately rummaged through a glove compartment filled with Canadian Tire money in a line at a drive-thru.

27. You can name more than one "Luba."

28. You've never won a Grand Slam tennis tournament.

29. The fact that some of the victims of the Titanic disaster are buried in Nova Scotia is a source of pride.

30. You know that "PFK" is Kentucky Fried Chicken in Quebec, and not the Kennedy brother that nobody talks about.

31. You need a list like this to explain to you what it means to be Canadian.

Hey, Mike: Although an "un-Canadian" statement, it is not unreasonable to say that Canadian singers and more importantly songwriters are among (if not are) some of the finest in North America. Artists such as Leonard Cohen, Joni Mitchell, Neil Young, k.d. lang, Celine Dion, Sarah McLachlan, Alanis Morissette, Shania Twain, among others, have proven to be highly popular, as well as influential outside of Canada. However, there are also a number of actors and comedians who have been equally successful and influential; again within a large group are Alan Alda, Michael J. Fox, Dan Akroyd, Martin Short, John Candy, and Jim Carrey. What are your thoughts/conclusions? Is it realistic to identify Canadian entertainers on a higher level? Or is this simply an ethnocentric conclusion? I realize that I have left out a number of other entertainers, Pamela Anderson, for instance (although I question the quality of her skills much more than I question the quality of her, um, "refined image"), as well as numerous writers and artists. What, if any, are the experiences and/or characteristics, qualities, realities of our culture, national will, and experience that elevate the Canadian standard?

SINCERELY, MICHAEL L.

This e-mail was obviously intended for somebody at the CBC.

Hey, Mike: Do you ever go to L.A. and hang with your brother, Pat?

SANDRA, MEDICINE HAT

My friends, Sean and Al, and I went to visit my brother in Los Angeles after he started doing really well — I didn't want to go see him when he wasn't. I was too afraid he'd ask for money. So we went for two weeks. First of all we rented a car, or to be more specific, I rented a car. I just wasn't allowed to drive it because Al does all the driving no matter where we go. So then we drove all around Malibu looking for Johnny Carson's house, with no map and no directions — Al refused to ask for directions. So we drove around. "What do you expect to see, Al? A big neon sign that says 'retired talk show host lives here!'?"

I just wanted to eat. So we got out of the car and started a huge fist fight right beside a ten-metre ravine and I punched Al and he almost toppled over the side. Then a tour bus full of tourists drove by and stopped to look, so we went for lunch.

All I had on were bathing shorts and a T-shirt so we decided to go to the Beverly Center to go shopping and look for celebrities. There were two old ladies in the information booth and I went up to ask them where the best place to look for celebrities was. So while I was talking to the two old ladies, Sean ran up behind me and pulled my shorts down. I was in such shock that, rather than reaching down and pulling them up, I spun around to get Sean. Of course, when I looked around I could see about a hundred people stopping to stare at me, so I pulled on my shorts and ran out of the mall. I could hear the laughter of those two idiots I generously call friends behind me. So I kept running, without any idea of where I was, but after forty or fifty minutes, I reached Pat's door and went inside. Later, Sean and Al drove up in the car, still laughing, trying to convince me that it was okay because no one knew who I was. My brother gave me his car for two days. I went sightseeing by myself. I spent the rest of the trip holding on to my pants.

THE CANADIAN WAY VS.
THE AMERICAN WAY

On the show we contrast Canadian and American society and culture with an arrogance we wouldn't display if we had American viewers. This is our most crowd-pleasing desk bit, because holding back applause and laughter during "Can–Am Way" would be construed by fellow audience members as unpatriotic.

When a blizzard hits in Canada, Canadians — Put flares, candles, blankets, and food in their car, put chains on their tires and drive, with extra caution.

When a blizzard hits in America, Americans — Take the day off.

If a group of paramilitary extremist cult members barricaded themselves in their compound and demanded an end to government intervention, Americans would — Send in the FBI and, if negotiations fail, use force.

Canadians would — Make them the loyal opposition.

*If aliens blew up the
White House —*
Americans would unite
together under a common
cause and defeat their
outerworldly enemy.

*If aliens blew up
24 Sussex Dr —*
The RCMP would show up
eventually and launch an
investigation.

*When Canadian postal
workers express anger over
their latest contract offer,
Canadians —*
Take it with a grain of salt.

*When American postal
workers express anger over
their latest contract offer,
Americans —*
Take cover.

*If an international incident
occurred involving two
foreign powers, Americans
would —*
Tune to CNN to further
apprise themselves of the
situation.

Canadians would —
Wait till the first period
ended and see what Don
Cherry had to say.

In America —
If a major entertainment
figure became involved in a
grizzly murder, there would
be wild speculation and
excessive media coverage.

In Canada —
There are no major enter-
tainment figures.

In America —
A good cup of coffee is still
worth about 70 cents.

In Canada —
The dollar is worth about
70 cents.

In America —
A really well made, critically acclaimed motion picture has a good chance of winning several Academy Awards.

In Canada —
A really well made, critically acclaimed motion picture has a good chance of being released.

Canadians travelling overseas —
Are treated as welcome friends from a distant land.

Americans travelling overseas —
Masquerade as Canadians.

In America when there's cold weather—
They blame it on a Canadian cold front.

In Canada —
There's no one to blame but ourselves.

In Canada —
Howie Mandel is considered an amusing fellow countryman.

In America —
He's worshipped as a god.

In Canada —
They're the life of Oktoberfest.

In America —
War criminals are deported.

In Canada —
We spell colour with a "u."

In America —
They spell it with a "k."

In Canada —
People look the other way when college athletes play a championship game.

In America —
People look the other way when college athletes commit crimes.

In Canada —
Bitter old Frenchmen bitch, moan, and generally make life miserable for the anglophones in Quebec.

In America —
They do the same thing in Florida.

In Canada —
Our leader's mouth is crooked.

In America —
Their leader's penis is crooked.

In America —
The National Enquirer is bought by millions who want the latest celebrity gossip.

In Canada —
Frank magazine is bought by an occasional, unsuspecting guy named Frank.

In Canada —
The brightest young actors are wanted in America.

In America —
The brightest young actors are on *America's Most Wanted*.

In Canada —
We're not proud of the fact that we have more than one famous woman named Luba.

In America —
They're not proud of the fact that more than one famous person skied into a tree.

In Canada —
A group of kids in hockey sweaters are on their way to practice.

In America —
A group of kids in hockey sweaters are on their way to a crack house.

In Canada —
Lake Ontario: Pristine and clear.

In America —
Lake Ontario: sludge-filled cesspool.

In America —
When a man assaults a total stranger in public, he's a deranged lunatic.

In Canada —
He's the prime minister.

In America —
1969 is referred to as the "summer of love."

In Canada —
69 is referred to as "dizzying heights for the dollar."

In Canada —
The nation's leader exposes himself to controversy while going abroad after a weather crisis.

In America —
The nation's leader weathers controversial crisis, exposing himself while going after a broad.

In Canada —
Forests are endangered by over-logging.

In America —
Forests are endangered by celebrities on skis.

In America —
A biathlon consists of skiing and shooting.

In Canada —
A biathlon consists of snowmobiling and swimming.

In America —
Dr. Kevorkian puts old people to sleep.

In Canada —
We have the Prime Network.

In America —
Millions watch *ER*.

In Canada —
Millions watch *ER*.

In Canada —
'67: Our last great year.

In America —
'67: The number of people accusing Bill Clinton of sexual harassment.

And for the sake of novelty ...

In Canada —
The surviving Dionne Quints received $4 million from the Ontario government.

In Britain —
Unfortunately, all five Spice Girls still surviving.

In Britain —
Soccer fans in stadium hurt by violence.

In Canada —
Soccer fans in stadium hurt by loneliness.

In Canada —
The majestic Rockies jut skyward in jagged formations.

In Britain —
So do their teeth.

Hey, Mike: Do people say stupid things to you because you're famous?

JAMES, CAT LAKE, ONTARIO

Why, yes, James, they do. But I've also done that, so I don't worry about it. Let me tell you a little story. My brother Pat opened for Jay Leno in Toronto's Massey Hall in 1983. Pat got me backstage passes but he warned me not to say anything stupid. So after the show, I went back to meet Jay. I was in such awe of him that when he came over I wouldn't look up at him. He shook my hand, and I said, "I think *American Hot Wax* is the finest film ever made." Jay quietly took his hand away and moved over to where Pat was standing and mumbled, "Your brother either has bad taste in comedy or he's retarded."

Hey, Mike: How do you get into stand-up? Is it something you're born with?

FRANK, FRENCH RIVER, ONTARIO

Getting into stand-up comedy was an easy decision. Short of my little three-month stint as a cop, my only job was as a Bell telephone installer. Let me describe a typical February workday. Up at 5:30 a.m., awake an hour later. Get into a freezing-cold van, drink a lot of coffee, smoke even more cigarettes. Receive first order, drive to location. Hang wires and tools from every available buckle on my uniform. Climb fifty-metre pole. Splice and connect wires for about two to three hours. Come down pole. See doctor re: frostbite and hypothermia. Go to bed, wake up next day, and repeat.

The first time someone laughed at something I said, I phoned Yuk Yuk's and signed up for amateur night. I never had any jokes, barely an act. Just the "Where are you from? What do you do?" It's not that I couldn't write a joke; in fact, I co-wrote my brother Pat's stand-up act before I even got into it. But as far as jokes were concerned, I could never get comfortable doing my own. It felt weird repeating the same line night after night, although it might have been my material. Here's a sample: "Do gay people have signs over their fireplaces that say 'Homo Sweet Homo'?" "Bungee jumping, the new fad. Wait till the Japanese get ahold of it. It'll be cordless." "I'm afraid of death: Dave Death, my goofy next door neighbour." Actually, after seeing it written down, that bungee cord joke is not so bad. No matter. I dropped the jokes, kept talking to the audience, and became a staple among Yuk Yuk's emcees. The whole time, I never left Bell. I got moved around quite a bit. Probably too much joking around for the corporate world. In the end, I was placed in the most appropriate job in the company. Sort of the Bell Internal Affairs. I turned in people who were ripping off the company. I loved it.

Hey, Mike: Remember the unemployment snitch line? Why did they cancel that?

JUST CURIOUS, MONTREAL

Remember it? I invented it. It was my idea! That was one of my best ideas ever! It worked for Bell Canada, it worked for the Peel police department, and best of all it worked for me! But I wanted it to be more, much more than just a UI snitch line. It was part of a grand scheme involving the Internet and cash prizes for successful convictions thanks to your calls. So that a sample call would be: "That's right, officer, it's me again, and it's a lot worse now. He's cheating on his UI, right? But it's worse than that. I think he's having an affair, he doesn't lift the toilet seat, and when he moved in I gave him a plant and I didn't get so much as a thank-you note! Cut him off! Give him a ticket. Lock him up!"

Hey, Mike: You seem pretty pleased with yourself. My mother says you must be a narcissist. Is that what you are?

SUSAN N.

Susan, I'd love to be a narcissist. I just don't think I'm good-looking enough. But maybe I am. I don't know. I'll have to think about that. Am I a narcissist? Hmm, let me think about that....

Hey, Mike: Why are all these women complaining that they're not being treated the same in the Olympics? I mean there's women's hockey, women's soccer, women's everything. What's next — women's boxing? What do you think?

DEREK M., BURNABY, B.C.

Synchro to the death. That's what I'm waiting for, Derek.

Dear Mike: How did you get your start as a comedian? Did you go to amateur nights at Yuk Yuk's?

IAN C.

Everyone always asks me how I started out as a comedian. Like a lot of other people, I started out by wanting to make my mother laugh. But my mother wouldn't laugh, so I had to tie her to a chair and tickle her until she went pee. Same with Grandma. This would go on for hours. It was funny until somebody went too far. That would be me. After a couple of hours Grandma would want her pills, so I used to balance them on her nose to torment her — Forget it Ian. I'm sick of telling how I started in comedy.

Hey, Mike: I notice that you're always blinking and touching your ears and nose. My father, who's a doctor, says that this indicates a nervous and compulsive person. Why are you so nervous?

SUSAN N.

You're not mad at me, Susan, you're mad at your mother for not standing up to your father. And you're mad at your father for being a drunk. Happy New Year!

Hey, Mike: I'm a big fan of the show but I have a question. What's in the cup on your desk? I heard it was lemon gin but my girlfriend said she saw you at a party and you only drink Diet Coke. Which is it? And when do you think people should start drinking?

TERRENCE W., EDSON, ALBERTA

Lemon gin? Do adults even drink lemon gin? I remember that my producer used to call it panty-remover. But that doesn't explain why he keeps wanting me to drink it.

According to my mother, a good time to start drinking is noon. And in terms of what age to start drinking, well, that's up to each of us. Basically, the Bullard family rules of drinking haven't really changed since I was thirteen. It's quite simple: You get a friend with a moustache to go into the beer store for you. Failing that, you go to the liquor cabinet (or, in my family, liquor bucket), mix four or five kinds of stolen liquor in an empty and (very important) cleaned peanut butter jar, and water the liquor bottles to replace what you steal. Then, making sure it's quite far below zero in temperature and wearing only a jean jacket for a coat, you go down behind the school or to the railway tracks and stand there for an hour in the freezing cold and force the liquor down your throat. When you start to slur your words or stagger or cry about your absent girlfriend, you're ready to go to the dance or to the party or, in the case of my parents, to the Rotary Club meeting. That's pretty much the way it's been in my family for generations, and that's why I don't drink.

Hey, Mike: Okay, now let me make sure that I've got this story straight. From what I understand, you used to work at Bell Canada, presumably behind a desk. Not too sure how many years that took up. However, tuning into your show, it appears that the time spent behind a desk at Bell has paid off in big dividends for you — now that you sit behind a desk for CTV/The Comedy Channel. My question is: Did you find the time spent behind the desk at Bell to be beneficial in your move to CTV? If so, I've been behind a desk at Bell for years — where can I apply for your job?

Here's more proof that your theory is correct: I also sat behind a desk in grades one through thirteen.

I actually think that the reason so many comedians want to host a talk show is that they never had a desk job. Many have never even held a day job. They figure that the desk gives them a respectability they never had when they worked Saskatchewan roadhouses.

There's not much dignity for touring comics. I vividly recall an early gig opening for Canada's foremost prop comic, who did his best to dazzle a small and indifferent group at this nightclub in eastern Ontario. As usual, he worked up a profound sweat while sending his hand-crafted toys, prosthetics, and supermarket-product parodies flying through the air in all directions. After he left the stage to negligible applause and the show ended, he had to return to collect his debris. Only, the stage had now become the dance floor. The evening's star attraction absorbed countless clogs to his temple while crawling around on his hands and knees looking for his act. Always the team player, I offered to help, but he declined because the props had to be retrieved and packed in a specific sequence (in case the following night's crowd took an interest in comedy).

Hey, Mike: I saw David Crosby on the show saying that he thinks an American network will steal you away. Another Canadian comedy genius about to conquer America. John Candy, Jim Carrey, Mike Myers ... Mike Bullard. I was wondering why you think Canadians are so funny?

MATT L., EDMONTON, ALBERTA

Ever since the SCTV craze in the early eighties, the media has loved to ask this question. Then they always give the answer: "Canadians have access to both American and British media, giving us a unique outsiders' perspective on pop culture." Also, they tell us, "Canadian talent gets to hone its craft in relative obscurity so that they're really polished when they get to Hollywood, whereas Americans are thrown into the spotlight too quickly." I've seen this stuff written in the paper and discussed on *Canada AM* constantly for almost two decades. I've seen fellow comedians interviewed on TV, and they give the same answers as above because they heard them on TV when they were growing up. This is how Greek and Roman myths survived — they were passed down from generation to generation.

Now you're going to get the real answer to the question "What makes Canadians so funny?"

Nothing, really. If you look at the most influential comedians of the past quarter-century — Jerry Seinfeld, David Letterman, Jay Leno, Garry Shandling, Dennis Miller, Steve Martin, *et al.* — one thing strikes you immediately. They're Americans. Canada has a tenth of the English-speaking population of North America, so it stands to reason that we'd have about a tenth of the famous comedians, and that's about what we have.

In the twenty years since SCTV, whose original cast was actually half American, Jim Carrey and Mike Myers have been the only super-successful Canadian sketch players. The Kids in the Hall had to settle for cult status in the U.S. although any one of them could break out at any time. Phil Hartman was born here, but he was as Canadian as Bob Hope was British. On the stand-up side, I can't think of anyone other than Howie Mandel and Norm Macdonald who really made an impact.

Compare that to the way Canadian women have dominated music, with Celine Dion, Shania Twain, Alanis Morissette, Sarah McLachlan, and now Deborah Cox. Or how Canadians have completely infiltrated American news broadcasting, with Peter Jennings, Morley Safer, Robert MacNeil, Kevin Newman, J.D. Roberts, Keith Morrison, Sheila MacVicar, Hilary Brown, and countless others. I always thought the most thorough case of

Canadian domination was in the field of game show hosting: Monty Hall, Jack Barry, Jim Perry, Alex Trebek, and the greatest of them all, Pat Bullard. It's about time for a national discussion on "What makes Canadians such great game show hosts?" I think it has to do with our unique outsiders' perspective.

As for comedy, get a load of this. Jay Leno, America's ratings leader at 11:30 p.m., comes from Boston. Conan O'Brien, America's ratings leader at 12:30 a.m., also comes from Boston. And Adam Sandler, the star of North America's top-grossing comedy movie of 1998, also comes from Boston. Jonathan Katz, Denis Leary, Colin Quinn ... the list goes on. I haven't seen one article about what makes Bostonians so funny. But if there ever is one, it'll be followed by about ten thousand more.

Yes, there are a lot of Canadian comedians making a living in the U.S. There are also a lot of Canadian doctors and engineers down there. I guess the lesson is that if you're Canadian and you're pretty good at something, there's money to be made in the States. If I went to the States and flopped, I'd probably still make more money than I do as a Canadian talk show host.

For the first time in my recollection, a newspaper recently referred to the exodus of Canadian comedians as a "brain drain." With all due respect to my old colleagues from the clubs, that is generous. I've seen these guys trying to read a road map. In any case, it shouldn't really bother Canadians if our comedians go south ... hell, it's the Canadian Dream. But our doctors and engineers are a different story, because taxpayers subsidize their education. I've never heard this discussed before, but educated professionals should have to work here for a certain number of years or else be required to pay back the thousands of dollars in subsidies they got from our government. Why the hell should we pay to train America's physicians? Oh, yeah, to look after David Crosby.

Hey, Mike: I'd just like to say I thought it would be great if you were to have Our Lady Peace on the show. I watch regularly and you've been getting better and better. By the way, I hope Tom Green is banned from the show now. Some of his stuff is funny, but he goes too far other times.

The band most often requested via e-mail is easily Our Lady Peace. It reflects quite badly on their career prospects that, after the best year they've ever had, people still view them as realistic *Open Mike* guests. I mean, I'm sure people would *really* love to see Bruce Springsteen or the Rolling Stones on our show, but we get very few e-mails to that effect. We don't even get Tragically Hip requests very often, so, even by Canadian standards, it's pretty clear that OLP is perceived as second-tier. It's quite unfair when you consider that they sold out Maple Leaf Gardens.

Tom Green is not banned from the show. He's banned from several shopping malls, zoos, beaches, and supermarkets, but he's always welcome at *Open Mike*. He's possibly the only nonmusical guest who draws his own crowd to the show. His crowd is young and energetic, and there's no way that's a bad thing for us. As for his comedy, it's extremely funny to some people and not at all to others. The debate rages within our own crew: Some think he's another Andy Kaufman, while some think he's just a purveyor of shock.

His third appearance on our show was our most talked-about episode ever. That was the one where he whipped out a dead raccoon from a garbage bag. We had to stop tape briefly so I could vomit, after which I quickly cut his segment short. At the beginning of the following segment, during my introduction of the Rheostatics, his encroachment into my personal space led me to grab him and throw him to the ground.

Here is a quick summary of Tom's history with *Open Mike* in his own words:

Visit One: The Bag of Milk

I just wanted to do some funny stuff but I was nervous because all the Comedy Network people were there. But I enjoyed the experience. I didn't want to piss anyone off because I love the show and I wanted to come back. I didn't think I'd ruin a microphone. [For the record, the microphone survived.]

Visit Two: The Sweater

The next visit was fairly tame. I talked about my shirt
and stuff. I didn't want to splash milk around this time. I
wanted a different sort of humour. I didn't want to be
throwing stuff around every time. After that show, people
were disappointed. "You weren't as crazy as last time,"
that kind of thing. But I was worried about the broken
microphone and the security.

Visit Three: The Raccoon

I thought the third time was pretty strong. We'd just got back from a road trip. I didn't think that a dead raccoon would be that outrageous. I was coming from another place. A ten-week road trip. I was in this mode of flow. We get in these modes of flows, and dead raccoons don't seem that crazy. I had a lot of fun.

I wasn't really surprised by the outcome. I was trying to do something to watch on television. The thing that was weird about that appearance was that it was a sort of major thing that made me realize what it is that I do. I was never referred to as a shock comic before in Canada. No one referred to me as a shock comic. I personally thought it demeaned what I do. It's ten percent milk, ninety percent the reaction of the people. Nobody in the U.S. calls it shock comedy. It was upsetting that the

Toronto Sun's first impression was "dead raccoon." It was a turning point because we didn't want to tip the scales too much in that direction.

Visit Four: Chainsaws and Flowers

The fourth appearance was the best. It was a lot longer. It was weird. Neat. And I improvised with Mike. That was good. I was actually more nervous about this appearance, though. I didn't want to do something rough. I wanted to say hello. I want my show to air in Canada and I wanted people to understand that it was coming to Canada. I felt guilty about the ten shows that my fans hadn't seen. It was an opportunity I had to take. I think it went pretty well.

We asked Tom why he didn't pull a stunt like the raccoon on Letterman.

You know, doing every show is different. Doing *Open Mike* is different from doing Letterman. And doing *Regis & Kathie Lee* is different again. Letterman is not the right forum for the raccoon. The pre-interview process is about the same. They knew I'd be talking about the limo. I gave them ten stories and used three. I listened for about twenty seconds to Letterman talking and I felt like I was going to black out. It was like an out of body experience. Doing Letterman is not like doing any other show for me. The big reason I do what I do is from watching Letterman when I was fourteen years old. He was my first U.S. interview.

Hey, Mike: There are lots of rumours flying around about what you're actually going to be doing on your hiatus. Could you please help to clear the air by confirming or denying some of these rumours.

1. You're going to be finishing the last few assignments needed to get your high school diploma.

2. You're going to get your "Anne Murray" tattoo removed.

3. You're going to be travelling around B.C. on the Moffatts' tour bus, acting as their spelling tutor.

4. You're going to drop in on those guys at Sportsnet and get even.

5. You're going to be the guest lecturer at the Ralph Benmergui School of Journalism while Ralph is busy out on the picket line.

6. You're not actually going on hiatus; it's just that you and Orin are switching places and you don't want people to watch in case he's better than you.

CRAIG, MISSISSAUGA

E-mails like this confuse me. You obviously want to be funny and have written a "bit" for me. I appreciate that. Yet you end with a "dig" at me. Do you have problems with authority, Craig? Maybe the relationship with Dad wasn't so hot? You make fun of my education and then use a semicolon properly. You know, Craig, I think I'm going to have to put you in my "ashamed to watch Bullard" category. Don't worry; there are many more like you out there. I realize that it's confusing for educated Canadians to find an "Anybody from out of town?" comedian funny. That's okay, Craig. You're allowed to like people from other classes. Hell, you're even allowed to try to write bits for them in your smarmy way. But next time, leave Ralph out of it. He had enough trouble with you the first time around.

Hey, Mike: I was just wondering: How come your band is called Orin Isaacs and the Open Mike Band? Why can't it be Tony Padalino and the Open Mike Band??????

JENNIFER S., HAMILTON

Because Orin is the bandleader??????

Hey, Mike: I was watching Double Exposure on Saturday, and they had this hilarious spoof of you. Did you see it? What they did was have you say, "How you all doing tonight?" then chuckle with your left hand on your belly ... This was repeated four times, Then you started to complain to the audience that they were messing up your monologue ... Then you chuckled some more. Isn't that soooo YOU!

YOURS TRULY, GLEN H.

Hey, Glen, you're messing up my book. Where are you from anyway? Heh heh heh ....

HEY, MIKE: YADDA YADDA YADDA. I WATCH THE SHOW, THINK IT'S WONDERFUL ... ONLY ONE PROBLEM. WHY DO YOU GET SO VIOLENT ON E-MAIL NIGHT? MY SOON TO BE MOTHER-IN-LAW HAD TO BE HOSED DOWN AFTER SHE WATCHED LAST WEDNESDAY NIGHT. WE E-MAILED YOU CONCERNING YOUR DRESSING ROOM DOOR ... CALM DOWN, YOU'RE A CANADIAN; WE'RE NOT LIKE THAT!!

JAMIEJ2

You have to stop living in the past, Jamie. Diefenbaker is dead. Trudeau is almost dead. Chrétien has nine lives. And I AM CANADIAN.

Hey, Mike: 200 shows. My, how things have changed. I remember when you first came on the air, at the end of your shows you would get your picture taken with all the guests. You don't do that anymore?? Is it because you have run out of wall space in your office, filled with other celebrities, or are there too many pictures of yourself!?!?!?! Just wondering??

A VERY DEVOTED FAN, JEFF

Hmm. A three-parter. Okay here goes.

1. No, I don't do that any more.

2. I was the one taking pictures. If I was in every photo, there would be no room for anyone else's head.

3. And, no, the photos didn't go into my office. They went on the wall at Gretzky's.

Hey, Mike: I really think that guy from CTU Sportsnet is very funny and you should have him on more.

MARCEL L.

Well Marcel, I disagree. The only reason that guy gets on our show is because of those three little words that come before Sportsnet: CTV. And because he's on CTV and I'm on CTV and we both have the same sugar daddy, I might as well introduce him now because he's getting in this book whether I want him to or not. Ladies and gentlemen, dear reader — Darren Eckler.

Hey, Mike: So tell me, what else does Lindsey do besides introduce you, Mike? Nice gig if you can get it, eh!

RUDY, AJAX, ONTARIO

All Lindsey has to do all day is introduce me ... in the 154 languages in which our show is dubbed. Nobody arrives at work earlier or leaves later than Lindsey, or as she's known in the Republic of Congo, "Ikenglolok," which means "leather-clad waif."

But there's another issue arising from the question/accusation in Rudy's e-mail. Rudy has examined the Lindsey situation and come to the conclusion that she doesn't work very hard. He was so certain of this conclusion that he felt the need to proclaim it in a communiqué to our show, hoping that it would reach a wider audience by being read on the air. Why do people always assume they know all about other people's business?

Here's a guy who I presume has never met Lindsey and has no idea what she does all day, but nonetheless can declare that her contribution to our society is negligible. What an ignorant thing to do.

Movie critics do that sort of thing a lot. I have no problem with a critic saying whether they liked a movie, but when they start professing about what the filmmaker should have done differently they should be slapped in the face. They have no clue what constraints the director was under creatively or financially, or what kind of rationale went into whatever decisions were made. There is, however, one thing they should be able to figure out: that the director probably put much more thought into the creative decisions of his own movie than a reviewer from the *Chicago Sun Times*.

We've all been guilty of this sort of mindset at times, but I'm trying to reform myself. When Fox Television announced that Magic Johnson would be getting a late-night talk show, I knew immediately that it would tank within weeks. It was as ridiculous as putting Jay Leno in the NBA. My first instinct was: Just how stupid are these people? Everyone in the world knows this is going to fail, why don't *they*? If I had had their e-mail addresses, I definitely would've e-mailed them to say they're idiots.

While *The Magic Hour* was cancelled within weeks and racked up $10 million in losses, I now realize that the most I could ever do if I met the Fox people is ask why they did what they did. For all I know, they had good reasons. Maybe Magic paid them to let him do the show to fulfil some kind of dream. Maybe sponsors were so enthusiastic that they committed to covering the losses. Maybe they were physically coerced by organized crime figures. And maybe, just maybe, they really are a bunch of totally clueless idiots.

I know you're wondering what application this sermon has outside of movies and television. It applies to every-thing, my children. Don't yell at the bus driver for swerving, because he may be avoiding a fallen cyclist. If your Swiss Chalet order is late, don't bawl out the girl on the phone making $6.85 an hour, because it probably has nothing to do with her. And don't prejudge your middle-aged bachelor neighbour who always carries the naked mannequins into his house, because he could just be in the mannequin repair business. Or he could just be a collector.

Why am I so militant on this issue? Because one day last year a talk show host was walking down the street when a stranger approached and said, "Hey, your bit with the audience really sucked on Friday." What the stranger didn't realize was that the talk show host had made a solemn promise to Father Delvecchio that he would refrain from insulting the audience on Good Friday, the day of that particular show. The stranger's hurtful remark was born of pure ignorance, because not only did the talk show host not "suck," his performance on the episode in question reflected both his integrity and his piety.

Oh, one more thing. That talk show host was me.

What a book this is turning out to be!

Hey, Mike: Did I see you at IKEA last week?

No, you did not. But you probably saw my announcer, Lindsay, there. Lindsay is, I'm sorry to say, an IKEA junkie. What you don't see every night when she's announcing the show is behind the scenes at her desk, where there is a series of spoon holders, trivets, fancy shower rings, and pot hooks, Lindsay took me to IKEA once — she said we'd be there for fifteen minutes max. We were there for five hours! Lindsay got lost. I had to go back against the traffic to find her. She was just standing in the clock department with this weird look on her face going "From Victor to Arthur, online ..."

Hey, Mike: I watch your show whenever there is nothing else on TV. You're kind of lame and I just can't help but notice that your a fat white guy. Kinda funny, but still the fact remains, you're a fat white guy. But that's a good thing, I LIKE FAT WHITE GUYS. You know why? You're shameless, you have nothing to lose. If you do something stupid, you don't screw up your image, cuz it never existed in the first place. Anyways, I'd like to take this time and say hi to your mom, and all your sisters. So i'll watch your show next time there is nothing on tv.

YOUR TRULY, AN ADVOCATE OF FAT WHITE GUYS AROUND THE WORLD, ABDUL F.

Thank you for your insightful correspondence.

Incidentally, this trend of people calling me fat is not hurtful to me, nor is it mysterious. The e-mail always mimics what we do on the air. For a long time, I was criticizing my writers after every joke, so we got hundreds of e-mails urging me to fire the writers. I stopped criticizing the writers on the air, and the e-mails about them stopped. Now we do constant jokes about my weight, because they almost always get a laugh, so the e-mails all remark on my weight. You'd love to believe that people think for themselves, but they don't, and they never will. In fact I didn't even write this sentence.

I'm not all that fat. "Burly" is a lot more accurate. Our jokes make it sound like I'm Orson Welles or something.

That's because when you're on five nights a week for thirty-five weeks a year, you don't turn your back on a guaranteed laugh. A typical example came after St. Patrick's Day, when we thought it might be funny to have production assistant Derek Thompson deliver the cards for a desk bit while hung-over. He came on with green teeth, urging the crowd to keep the noise down. Nobody laughed. Then, continuing with the drunk theme, he challenged me to a fight in the parking lot. Muted laughs. Then, like breaking the glass to get the emergency fire extinguisher, Derek did what was necessary to save the day.

He yelled: "Mano a lardo!"

The crowd exploded in hysteria.

So, for the good of the show, I will continue to work with a personal trainer who force-feeds me KFC and hides the key to my treadmill.

Isn't it eerie that kids growing up in the 90s may not know what KFC stands for? We actually had an argument in the writers' room over why they changed it from Kentucky Fried Chicken to KFC. My understanding was that they believed the word "fried" to be a turn-off in an increasingly health-conscious society. But our head writer, who takes more than a superficial interest in fast food, claims that the U.S. courts had barred KFC from using the word "chicken." He said it was because their chickens were so altered by chemicals and other processes that they no longer had the properties of a chicken. I still disagree, but now I'm starting to wonder. You know how if you eat chicken wings and leave the bones lying around overnight, they start to smell? Well, I recently had KFC and, since my wife was out of town, I left the remains on the counter for a whole week. No rotting odour. You kids out there, feel free to use this idea for your next science project.

Hey, Mike: From the few shows I've watched, you seem to be obsessing over your unusually large cranium. Worry no longer. 23" is average. Be glad you're not Oprah. Hers is 25. P.S. When are you going to appear on your American counterparts' talk shows, i.e., Letterman, O'Brien, etc.?

RON, CHATHAM, ONTARIO

I'll stop doing jokes about my huge head the minute audiences stop laughing at them. Until then, my writers will continue to write punchlines by spinning a big wheel that stops on "fat," "bald," or "big head."

As for going on American talkshows ... out of pride, I refuse to appear on them until I get invited. It must be that Canadian politeness in me.

Hey, Mike: This has two parts: One, to the bass player ... Do you really dig that keyboardist in the band? Really? <wink, nudge> Be honest. Are those "patented" pitch bends his attempt at being cool, or is he searching for the key? The rest of the band smokes, however! One thing, though: maybe you could think about "fattening" your sound a bit, add some low-end soul? The bass sounds kind of metallic sometimes, not quite enough warm throb to my ears. Maybe you like it that way?!

To Mike ... I like how you used Wide Mouth Mason and the whole condom thing at their expense for the benefit of yourself and your show. The guy everyone loves to hate; it's a proven formula, and you wear it well. Sweet. By the way, didn't you think WMM kicked conscious? Let's see more bands who are trying to stretch the boundaries of pop.

FLUIDGROOVE

Finally, an e-mailer who really understands what they're talking about. Fluidgroove, if you're not already a professional producer, you should be. It seems like you know more about the inner workings of show business than people on our own staff. E-mail us back with your name and phone number if you're interested in working for Open Mike, perhaps as a creative consultant. We could really benefit from your input on a full-time or part-time

*Ah yes ... the old "you're an orphan and your parents
are llamas routine" ... it was funny every time ...
that one never got old!*

*Every Sunday night was performance night at my
house ... you can see where I got my inspiration ...
they practically pushed me into showbusiness.*

Here's an investigator from Ripley's who came to see me levitate pillows.

*That's me on my way to career day at school ...
I couldn't decide between football player,
milk man or eccentric playboy.*

There's my dad moments after I told him I wanted to get into showbusiness.

There's my mom ... same day, same conversation.

I remember thinking, how does a big fat guy with a beard get so popular?

There's my dad in his inventor phase ... he called it the boogie stool.

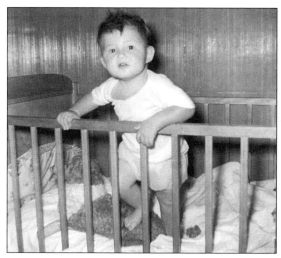

First time reading off cue-cards.

My dad told me he used to try and teach me to walk ... he also told me that my mom would say "once the little runt makes it across the room without falling get him a paper route!!!"

The story goes ... my grandmother lived in a haunted house ... apparently that stove would appear out of nowhere and start simmering a fish stew.

I'll never forget that weekend ... that was the first time I ... you know ... ate ten burgers off a plate with no hands ... I don't know who the girl is but I remember her getting in the way of the meat.

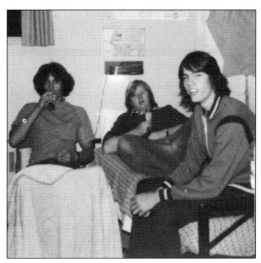

"That 70s Show"...
we had the idea long before anyone at Fox.

The very day I got "Open Mike" I went out and bought
my mom a brand new ... necklace.

That's me, every time the rest of
my family went on vacation.

*I was a silver
miner in the
Yukon in '78
... To make a
little extra
money I set
up a kissing
booth.*

basis, whenever you're available. One more thing, fluidgroove: FANTASY'S OVER, YOU PRETENTIOUS BLITHERER! You don't sound cool, you sound like a character from the movie Fame.

Hey Mike: Your show is great! I caught a taping when I was in T.O. for the Stones concert. The one with the freak show (that guy climbing out of the box) and Bob and David from Mr. Show. I liked the show so much I decided to attend the Junos that were hosted by you. We had great seats beside the stage, where you were hosting. I could see the teleprompter and was routinely watching it to see when you were immprovising. You were incredibly funny. Especially the jabs about hip-hop. That music is so boring, angry, and all sounds the exact same. Do the artists really believe that they are doing something different? This music is just a warm-up for their drive-by shoutings after the concerts. My question finally is two parts, at the junos were you improvising on stage or were you given comments to say before you got on stage? By looking at the teleprompter, the whole show was almost improv. If this was improv, well done, I must commend you on your performance, although there were some nine year old who would have clawed your eyes out, over the Moffatts (Hanson, media-hyped wannabes).

The second part, I hope this is not incredibly long and boring, is that, was there a screw-up at the beginning of the Junos when you were not reading from the teleprompter and introduced the first award being presented, was that for hip-hop or rap? The stage manager, the one for your show, was going crazy and everyone was scrambling!! Did anyone catch it? If you got this far, thanks for reading and please respond. Keep up the great work and see ya later.

CHRIS

For the most part, I don't know what Chris is talking about. However, in light of the fallout from my Junos appearance, I'd like to take this moment to reflect on the surprising percentage of Canadian celebrities who don't understand what a joke is.

I suppose it has something to do with the fact that we've never had a star system before. Now we do, and I'm proud that shows like *Open Mike* are in some part responsible. The people who benefit from the system will become stars. As stars, they are objects of adulation, quicker service in restaurants, endorsement offers, the odd death threat, and jokes.

For those of you who are stars in Canada, or hoping to someday be one, a joke is defined by the Oxford English Dictionary as "a thing said or done to excite laughter."

Note that it says nothing about "commenting" or "informing."

So, when I made jokes in the Junos monologue about the Canadian rap community, it was no reason for uproar. If anything, it should have been perceived as a sign that the rap community is gaining clout. If you take the rappers at their word, it was proof that Canadian rappers are not being taken seriously.

In case you missed it all, I made a variety of jokes in the opening monologue about the likes of myself, Moffats, Alanis Morissette, the CBC, and MuchMoreMusic. I have no beef with any of these entities.

I also said, with no malice or even interest, that we should be proud that, in all the years that the Junos have been honouring rap, there hasn't been a single fatality. I added that the worst we've had are a few drive-by shoutings. The basis for the joke was the startling number of homicides involving rap stars in the U.S. and the lack thereof in Canada. The result of the jokes was laughter from the audience at Copps Coliseum, and angry stares from the rap nominees in the front rows.

Later, when an amalgam of established Canadian rappers won the rap Juno, one of them by the name of Kardinal Offishall used part of the acceptance speech to say the following:

"We'd like to say to all the media out there: we want you to approach hip-hop music, and R&B music, reggae ... everything ... with the same type of humour that you did when you were making fun of hip-hop. Because, when you guys want to accuse gangsta rap of being the cause of all this violence, we'll be laughin' at you just like you were laughin' at us. So, you gotta be serious with this hip-hop. This is no joke."

A reasonable response would be: "I didn't understand a word of that."

But the tone of his delivery made it pretty clear he was indicting the monologue jokes as a brush-off of his craft. It would be rude of me not to respond:

1. I have no relative disregard for the Canadian rap community. I take it as seriously as I take Celine Dion, Shania Twain, and Bryan Adams. Which is not that seriously.

2. The Kardinal (whose appointment by the Pope shocked conservative Catholics) should only be concerned if he and his rap brethren are not mentioned in the Juno monologue.

3. It's ironic that I'm on the receiving end of this attack, because *Open Mike* was one of the first mainstream television programs to showcase rap performances on a regular basis. Kardinal Offishall was among our first musical guests in 1998.

4. I'm not too concerned about any of this, because a rapper being angry is not a big deal. In fact, it's sort of their job. It's my job to laugh at everything, and it's their job to get angry about everything. Then I go home and watch PBS documentaries on world over-population, while they go home and watch *America's Funniest Home Videos*. I'm sure of it.

When the Junos ended, there was a press conference where I was asked, "Would you be making jokes if it was country artists shooting and killing one another?" That might be the easiest softball ever lobbed my way. I just said, "Yes, and I look forward to that." Everyone laughed except the reporter who asked the question.

If you have any doubt that one line from a comedian can be the basis for a huge essay, you didn't see what the *National Post* wrote about my MuchMoreMusic joke from the Junos monologue. Here's the joke: "Canada has a new video channel, MuchMoreMusic, where they had some trouble on the weekend. Because of technical problems, they went eleven minutes without playing "Walking in Memphis." They got it fixed, but it was tense for a while."

Two weeks later, the *Post* came out with an article entitled "Walk on the Mild Side." Among other things, it said that "the joke was the first public suggestion that the six-month-old station has a narrow, boomer-oriented playlist, where nearly every selection can be traced within a few degrees of David Foster, aimed at an audience of advertiser-coveted young professionals." Actually, I was saying that the station plays "Walking in Memphis" a lot.

The article then featured a defence of MuchMoreMusic by its vice-president, Denise Donlon. It quoted her as saying that the MuchMoreMusic playlist is "a little more varied than Bullard's perception would indicate." I have a perception?

It got better: "Donlon admits to liking 'Walking in Memphis,' but she laughs and suggests the joke had more to do with Bullard's own musical tastes than the reality of the station. 'I know Mike picked that song because last time I talked to him he was upset about MuchMoreMusic ... since Tom Petty was on it, and it meant he was old, Mike Bullard was old."" We laughed for half an hour when we read that in the writers' room.

For the record, I am a big fan of MuchMoreMusic and I watch it constantly. Denise Donlon was one of our finer guests and is always welcome on our show. And our show continues to welcome Canadian rappers, who continue to accept our invitations.

In case you're wondering whether our show is shying away from rap violence jokes as a result of the Junos thing, here's something from my monologue the day after the Junos: "I hope the rap community wasn't upset about my jokes about rap violence ... because you really don't want to tick those people off."

One thing I've always wondered regarding rap is the need for fake names. I thought, If this art is so damn legitimate, why can't it be practised by "Fred Johnson" or "Jane Stackhouse" instead of "MC Kool" and "DJ Ice Kool" and "Grandmaster Kooly Kool"? By the way, I was shocked to find out that the holders of the MC and DJ designations don't have to pass any kind of written exam. So one day I saw on *Entertainment Tonight* that Will Smith was putting a rap album out under his own name. I was strangely excited. It was like years had been taken off my age. I thought: Yes! This is a perfectly normal person with a real name ... I don't have to feel alienated and confused by rap!

HEY, MIKE: NOW THAT YOU'RE A BIG SHOT IN THIS CITY, IS IT TRUE THAT YOU HAVE A PERSONAL BODYGUARD WHEN YOU WALK THE STREETS OF T.O.? P.S. WHAT THE HECK HAPPENS IF SOMEONE GETS TOO CLOSE?

CARLITO

Carlito, I've checked with my security guard and he's advised me not to speak to anyone who writes in all caps. Too dangerous for this big shot.

Hey, Mike: I want to know one thing. How does a guy get set up with his own talk show? And another thing: Tell those people at CTV that if they want to make money, you have to spend money. Like, come on, let's see about getting Orin a new set of shirts. Those things are nasty.

CARY O., BONNYVILLE, ALBERTA

Bonnyville? And you're criticizing Orin's shirts? Why not just come down to the studio and tell him yourself, because I ain't telling him. And neither is the network. Orin's very particular about his clothes and, well, we've just decided that it's better to let him have his way. Besides, we're scared of him. The man is a political machine. I suspect that if he reads this letter, your water is going to get cut off or your mother's going to lose her place in line for a hip replacement. The man has powers, Cary. Good luck, buddy.

Hey, Mike: Could you ask Orin to act more like Paul Shaffer? I think my life would be complete ... skinnier and, heh, what about pretending he can play on his knees ... or, heh, what about just saying HEH over and over and doing a little more high pitch with the voice or, HEH ... what about ... naw, forget it.

ANONYMOUS

Heh. Heh. We'll forget it.

Hey, Mike: The show is great but limited by the calibre of the monologue. Do you dream of the possibilities consistently funny monologues would bring? It would complete the package. I do have one complaint. When you read e-mails (Wednesday nights) you always tap the papers on your desk every few seconds. Last Wednesday, I counted over forty taps on the desk. This is so not necessary. The papers do not get messed up. It is just a bad habit that really annoys me.

MICHAEL S., CHARLOTTETOWN, PEI

Well, Michael, it really annoys the producers, too. TAP

Hey, Mike: I love the phone-in gag, but could you tell the characters to tone it down a little? Everyone knows that there aren't really people that stupid out there. Later.

SCOTT

Funny, that's what my editor said when I suggested we answer my e-mails and put them in a book.

Hey, Mike: I watch your show every day and frankly I am becoming obsessed with you. The only reason I watch your show is to see you. I think you are one of the sexiest men on the planet. Well, you and Orin. I'd appreciate it if you called me because I would love to speak to you in person. Call me at 902-***-****. And ask for James.

I called. What happened next is none of your business.

Hey, Mike: I have seen the CTV vignette with PMike tossing a round, red object up and down. What is the object and what does it mean?

It could be a tomato, and Mike is saying To Eat or Not To Eat, that is the Question.

1. Mike could be thinking of becoming a pitcher.

2. He could be an amateur juggler on his first lesson.

3. He could be a professional juggler who has lost two balls.

4. It could be that he couldn't think of anything better to do.

5. I think that he is just trying to make everybody wrack their brains figuring out what he is doing.

SCORPIO

IT WORKED! IT WORKED!

My parents were at your show a few months ago and gave to Mike a copy of a press release for the 1998 Canadian Cherry Pit Spitter. He said that the producer would be getting ahold of me. I am still waiting.

MARTIN S.

What's amazing is that it doesn't say here that he was the *champion* cherry pit spitter in Canada. He was just the *Canadian* spitter for 1998. I guess if you wanted cherry pits spitted in 1998, and you didn't want to hire a foreigner, you had to go to Martin.

I hear all the time from prospective talent, and I do forward all inquiries to the producers. In this case, they must have decided that cherry pit spitting wouldn't make for great television. I mean, there must be a reason we've never seen it on TSN.*

We had a woman walk into our offices recently announcing that she wanted us to do a segment with her pet ram. She stressed that her ram "is extremely friendly — except when he's ramming."

I said that I'd never actually seen a real ram with the horns and everything. She then told us that her ram doesn't have horns — some have them and some don't, and hers doesn't. I told her that I have a unicorn at home, but it doesn't have a horn. That's why some people think it's a dog, but it's really a unicorn.

---

*Bookers: In the fine spirit of people who want to come on our show, he didn't give us a contact number.

I guess it's possible that horns are not standard in all ram models, but they really oughta be. I forgot to ask the woman if her ram has other features like cruise control. Then we'd have a segment.

I don't know why everyone believes their pet belongs on television. We did a segment with my dog, Yankee, but that's only because he's exceptionally adorable and talented. Everybody on our staff thinks so, except for the two people I fired. I didn't fire them for not liking my dog, which would be maniacal behaviour on my part. I fired them because of their inability to recognize when a dog is so clearly phenomenal, suggesting a lack of analytical acumen so grave that they would be out of their depth in *any* job.

I can really fly off the handle when my dog isn't respected. I walked Yankee to a popular dog park recently. It's a forty-minute walk to get there, so Yankee was a little worn out when we arrived. As we all know, tired dogs tend to drool, and Yankee is no different. Hey, he's only canine.

So we were walking through the park and came upon a small group standing around. The group consisted of what appeared to be two fortysomething dads with a few young kids and a couple of dogs. As Yankee approached them, one of the dads — the entertainer of the group — said with a lilt in his voice: "Look at the goober coming out of *that* dog!" His brood laughed. I didn't say a word, because I was afraid I would scare his kids with my talk of homicide.

Because he was so clearly on a roll, he added: "That's a lot of goober!" More laughs. My blood was boiling. I knew that if I heard the word "goober" again, I would be unable to control my violence. I grimly said: "Come on, Yankee."

As we started to walk away, Dad says: "Yankee? That's a pretty upscale name for a dog with all that *goober*." I stopped for a split second. I was ready to hit this guy so hard that something other than goober would be pouring out of his mouth. And then, as though God were leading me by the hand, I kept walking. I guess I didn't want to leave any of the kids fatherless. Although I would've been doing them a favour. Who wants to grow up with a dad whose only comedic device is using the word "goober"?

Meanwhile, the only reason there was no "goober" coming from his dog was that they were just standing around. I walked Yankee for forty minutes just *getting* to the park, while this guy probably drove his dog there in a minivan and then stood around. Later, when I was walking near the park entrance, I saw him *carrying* his dog out of there. I'm serious. I'm too angry; we'd better move on to another subject.

Hey, Mike: Please have Joe Clark on again. He has been the best guest you have ever had. I bet you thought you were going to have a better conversation with a validated parking meter. Brother, did he nail you!!!!!!!!!!!!!!!!!!!!!!!!! Mike rocks!!!!!!!!!!!!!!!!!!!

CATCH YA ON THE FLIP SIDE. KYM B.

Remind me to avoid the flip side.

But Kym raises a good point. People often say: "You must've been excited having Lenny Kravitz on," or "Tracey Ullman — wow, you're getting real stars now."

However, the truth is, we're never going to match our American competitors for star power. Ninety-nine nights out of a hundred, Conan will have bigger stars than we do. The only way we can compete is by offering an alternative. It's a very compelling alternative when we present Canadian icons out of their regular environment.

For example, Conan may have actor Jeff Goldblum on, and we'll have CTV newscaster Sandie Rinaldo. Goldblum was in *Jurassic Park* and *Independence Day*, so we can all agree he's the much bigger star. But we've seen him on a million talk shows already. We've never seen Sandie Rinaldo away from the anchor desk. As a result, a quarter of a million Canadians will choose to watch the lesser star. And they're not disappointed, thanks to Sandie's disco-era memorabilia.

The ultimate example of our Canadian edge was the appearance of federal Tory leader Joe Clark, the only former prime minister to visit us thus far. Like the entire country, I was interested in finding out just how boring this man could be. Finally, like a dentist appointment you dread, it was time to introduce him.

That's when the sixteenth prime minister of Canada came out and knocked us all right on our asses.

And he wasn't a one-trick pony. He killed with prepared anecdotes, he killed with audience interplay, and, as Kym reminds me, he scored biggest with spontaneous shots at me. I'm not anxious to have him back quickly, because our ridiculously low expectations have been replaced by ridiculously high expectations. It's much more fun to relive his flawless first visit, which is probably not done justice in written form. Nonetheless, here's a partial transcript. Keep in mind that, even for an experienced comedian, three or four "applause breaks" constitute a very successful segment.

Me: Joe, you retired from politics in 1993. Five years later, here you are back. What prompted that decision?

Joe: Well, you worked in the telephone business once, didn't you?

Me: Yes, I did, as a matter of fact.

Joe: Well, I was sitting at home in Calgary. I'd been there three years, waiting for the phone to ring after I left Parliament. One day it rang, and the woman on the other end said, "Can I speak to Mr. or Mrs. R.T. Hon?" I said, "I'm sorry, there are no Hons here." She said, "Sir, this is your telephone company. This telephone is registered to Mr. and Mrs. R.T. Hon, and I want to speak to them." My title, you might remember, is the Right Honourable — Rt. Hon. So I said, "What was it that you wanted to talk to Mr. and Mrs. Hon about?" And she said, "I'm with the Special Services Bureau of the Unlisted Telephone Numbers Division of Alberta Government Telephones, and I wanted to tell you about the special services you could have as a holder of an unlisted phone number." And I said, "You know, I sort of thought as a holder of an unlisted telephone number, one of the services I would have is that people like *you* wouldn't call me." (Joe's first applause break.) So the reason I came back, Mike, is so that people would call.

Me: So that you could share that kind of personal charm with *all* of us?

Joe: I'm glad you noticed that. My first time in public life, I struggled and struggled — nobody saw the charm. I thought: If there's an expert in charm whom I could consult, who would it be? So here I am. (Applause break #2.)

Me: You've certainly received a warm welcome here tonight. But as you've travelled across Canada, what's been the reaction toward the fact that you're back?

Joe: When I started years ago, the *Toronto Star* — a little local newspaper — celebrated my arrival in public life with a great big headline that said "Joe Who?" I'll never forget that. Things are much better now. One out of every six hundred people recognizes me right away. Although, I was down in Prince Edward Island this summer — (a few people clap) — the whole *island's* here! (Applause break #3.)

Me: Oh, Joe, I'm starting to wonder why I never voted for you.

Joe: If I might just say — this small commercial announcement: there's still time. There's still time for all of you.

(Joe tells P.E.I. story, which yields applause break #4.)

Me: You want to be prime minister again, I take it. There's no shame in admitting it.

Joe: What I wanted to do was get on this show. (Applause break #5.)

Me: May I say something — you thought it was "Joe Who" *before*.

Joe: Yeah, I'm here to go back to being prime minister, and I really wanted to check you out 'cause I heard that you were gonna lead the Unite the Right movement.

Me: Yeah, that's right.

Joe: I'd stop right now.

Me: The interesting thing to me is, take a look at you, Joe Clark, and Jean Chrétien. You have the same initials. And Preston Manning—PM: prime minister.

Joe: Or post-mortem. (Applause break #6.)

Me: Five years off sure didn't keep you political, did it?

Joe: No, but see, you weren't paying attention before. I've always been like this.

Me: I had no idea.

Joe: People thought that I was as dull as a guy who worked for a telephone company. (Applause break #7.)

Me: Preston Manning was here about three weeks ago. I asked him, "What would you say to Joe Clark if you saw him here?" and he passed along some words of wisdom and said that he was going to call you. Did you ever get a telephone call from Preston Manning?

Joe: You have no influence.

Me: He didn't call, huh?

Joe: I was wondering why, and I'm sure it's your fault. No, he didn't call.

Me: I don't blame myself. We all know how you react when the telephone rings, Joe. Are the two of you going to get together and try to resolve your differences?

Joe: Well, not if you're in the race.

Me: I won't be, Joe.

Joe: You won't be in the race?

Me: No, I'm very happy here and I make a lot more money than you do.

Joe: Yeah, I was thinking about that and, y'know —
you're not as funny as I am. (Applause break #8.)

Me: You got that right, you got that right. Okay, I want
to thank you very much for coming. I know you've
got a busy schedule and you have to go now. You
don't *really* have to go, but I want you gone now, Joe.
Thank you very much for coming by.

Hey, Mike: Do you ever notice that those politicians, entertainers, or other "WWF freaks" with right-wing, American, or extremist agendas always get to explain their politics to an audience. Yet famous people holding traditional Canadian values never seem to get the same type of forum. Sure it's assumed we all know, but that assumption ignores young or new Canadians still learning, and denies the rest of us healthy affirmations of our beliefs! Mike, you have a great opportunity to give Canada a voice, and we could all use the odd reminders of what's made us great. Thanks. Keep slagging those Americans!!!

ANONYMOUS

This kind of letter disgusts me. How can you equate
"right wing" and "extremist" with "American"? As far as
I'm concerned, we're damn lucky we've got the U.S.A. on
the other side of that border and not Germany or China.
Can you imagine a country with such firepower never

once threatening our Confederation, even though we've taken an opposing stance on issues like Cuba and fisheries?

The United States isn't perfect, which is why we can do a regular desk bit called "The American Way vs. The Canadian Way." (That bit also preys on Canadian imperfections.) But until the day they're amassing tanks at the Peace Bridge, it's ridiculous to think of them as anything but a great friend. You can question their association with some evil regimes around the world, but Canada has similar associations. Plus, we've sold nuclear technology and carcinogenic asbestos to Third World countries.

Oh, sure, the U.S. has problems with violence and racism that we can only pray never gain a foothold here. America also looks dirtier to me. Their private spaces, like malls and stadiums, are gleaming and opulent. But they have a stunning lack of pride in public property like roads and parks. When you cross the border to Niagara Falls, New York, you're amazed to see that every lamppost is leaning, and it appears that there's rust on things that aren't even metal (unless you're on a toll highway). Whenever I travel in the U.S., or anywhere else for that matter, I'm always relieved to return to Canada.

Of course I'll read it. But not on the air, on account of its pointlessness.

But this brings up an interesting topic: making fun of Canadian regions. There was a time, back in 1997, when we really did have about four viewers in B.C. Our producers were completely unwilling to let us mock anybody outside of Toronto so as not to offend. Ironically, that led to accusations that we were too "Toronto-centric."

Back then, there was a news story that moisture was found on the surface of Mars, suggesting that there may be life there. I wanted to say: "I don't know about that — there's plenty of moisture in Vancouver, and there's no life there." My producer, Al Magee, and I decided there's no way that we could say that. American talk shows do jokes about inbreeding in the southern states, and I couldn't say that Vancouver is lifeless. That's when I quit, and was replaced by my twin brother, Larry, who continues to host the show to this day. Perhaps I've said too much.

But it is a fine line. Two weeks later we included the following joke as part of a desk bit called "Eerie Similarities." "The U.S. Prison Population and the people of Vancouver both number about 1.8 million, both are on drugs, and both get about an hour of sunlight a day."

That's the bit that prompted my remark that we have only four viewers in B.C.

Our new policy is similar to that of journalists: If you get an equal amount of hate mail from all sides, then you're doing your job. We've gotten angry letters from B.C. and Newfoundland, and from most points in between. Most of our jokes are about Toronto, but they never complain, because they have no inferiority complex. Toronto is to the regions of Canada what the U.S. is to the whole world: a big, welcoming, multicultural work-horse that sends money all over the place, yet somehow gets labelled "insular" and "greedy."

Newfoundland seems to have a pretty good sense of humour about everything, but there was a point in late 1998 when they were getting pretty upset over our constant insults. I finally went on the air and spoke directly to Newfoundlanders, pledging to stop the mockery because "I don't want any more death threats, or as you've been writing, 'det treets.'" I know that's not brilliant, but not all fun TV moments are.

To my dismay, we still have to turn down gems occasionally. Take this one. "Tomorrow marks the fiftieth anniversary of Newfoundland joining Canada. The federal government is paying for a big party — which pretty much sums up the fifty years." We thought it was "too cruel" to do on their big anniversary.

By the spring of 1999, we turned our attention to Montreal. After five months of mourning the loss of comedy caused by the rejuvenation of the Toronto Maple

Leafs, we finally woke up and realized that people laugh even harder when it's the arrogant Montreal Canadiens in last place. The first joke couldn't have been simpler: "Montreal was paralyzed when striking city workers refused to salt the roads after they froze over. It was especially hazardous for Montrealers who have trouble functioning on ice, like the elderly, people in wheelchairs, and the last-place Canadiens." The place went nuts. Our head writer, Lawrence Morgenstern, noted that this was the first time in his twenty years doing sports comedy in Canada that the standard "this team sucks" jokes were being applied to the Habs.

So we did an "Eerie Similarity" comparing the Montreal Canadiens to fermenting grapes: "Both stink, both get stomped, both are obsessed over by the French, and both will end up in the cellar." The reaction of the crowd transcended comedy. They were enjoying the tables being turned. Not all of our viewers enjoyed it, though, as proven by the next e-mail.

Hey, Mike: You are a fat c*#$!#!er. How dare a bald goof such as yourself insult the habs. Let me guess, you are a make me laugh fan (in case you don't know, that's the maple leafs). Are you proud to be a fan of a team who had people in the head office raping little children?? Yeah, there's a team to be proud of. GO MAPLEFILES GO!!!! You are not a true hockey fan, are you? If you cared to take the time to do some research instead of just throwing a bunch of trash together for your show, you would have seen that the habs have a MUCH better record than the leafs, so maybe you should be calling them the bottom dwellers. You are a no-talent loser who only got the job because they couldn't reach Mike McDonald over the phone. Your jokes are lame and you'll never be a Jay Leno or a David Letterman. Give up your career now before you get canned, you fat bald loser!!

A VERY BIG HABS FAN!!!!

Since the Leafs were doing well and the Habs were dead last, we were able to conclude that the scholar who wrote this e-mail was referring to cumulative team histories when he said "the habs have a MUCH better record than the leafs."

But that didn't stop us from reading that line on the air and responding as follows: "I guess I owe this person and all the Montreal fans an apology. Here are the current standings." We then displayed that day's NHL standings from the newspaper, which showed Montreal in last place.

"As you all know, I don't really follow hockey and have to rely on the information I get from my staff, who mistakenly told me that the team at the bottom of the standings is doing the worst. That information was obviously wrong. Montreal is doing great. And I thank our e-mailer for clearing this up. In fact, let's put those standings up again just to set the record straight." We showed the standings again on the full screen.

"Again, I apologize, I didn't realize that being on the bottom is a sign of success in hockey. And Montreal has been there all season and is clearly staying there. They're doing so well, I'm told, that they're being awarded an early vacation to begin in April, while other teams like the Leafs are being forced to play on — until they get it right, I guess. So congratulations, Montreal! Enjoy your well-deserved vacation."

The crowd really enjoyed that. My only concern was that maybe the big Habs fan wasn't watching that night to enjoy it as we did. That concern was unwarranted.

Hey, Mike: Looks like you have went and done it again!!! Next time you choose to use my e-mail READ THE WHOLE DAMN THING, not just the parts you feel the need to read. Now, if you had a brain you would have realized in my last e-mail that when I said just look at the record I meant the habs TOTAL record compared to the maple leafs. NOT JUST THIS SEASON!!!! Dummy. Do you realize that in the past thirty years this will be the habs second time missing the playoffs??! I bet not. Now go do some research and see how many times the leafs have made it into the playoffs!! Oh, and by the way, who holds the record for the most cups?? Oh, wait a minute, would that be the habs???? I believe so!!! Quit making fun of the habs. They are a great time [Ed: I think he means team.] with a great history!! I don't see you putting down the leafs. Now why is that, Mike??

A HABS FAN

When you see this guy's futile combination of anger and frustration, do you think at all of Yosemite Sam? I do for some reason.

Here's how I read this e-mail on the air:

"Hello, Michael. Next time you choose to use my e-mail, READ THE WHOLE DAMN THING, not just the parts you feel the need to read. Now, if you had a brain you would have realized BLAH BLAH BLAH, BLAH BLAH BLAH ... Quit making fun of the habs. I don't see you putting down the leafs. Now why is that, Mike?"

Then I said, "Oh, here's why." We put up the standings again. I wondered if we'd ever hear from this guy again. Probably not, I thought. Surely he's too busy with his many productive endeavours.

Hey, Mike: Thought I would give your show another chance seeing as you are Canadian, but nothing has changed with you!!! You admit to not knowing anything about hockey so why insist on insulting the habs?? Why aren't you bugging the maple files??? The habs are not DEAD last-look again!!! (I'm talking about overall in case you are too stupid to see that.) Hey, Mikey, were you part of the maple leaf organization??? Is that why you love them so much?? Shame on you!!! You're going to hell!!! Once again, before you go insulting the habs take a look at the records between the habs and the maple files. OVERALL, MIKEY, NOT JUST THIS SEASON!!!! I'll have the last laugh when your "oh so mighty leafs" get beat out of the playoffs and, yes, I know that the habs aren't making it this year. Second time in thirty years!!! Can you say that about the leafs?? I bet not!!!!

LOYAL HAB FAN

I'm sure he'd still be writing if he didn't have to go hunt "varmints."

Hey, Mike: I wanted to tell you what a funny name is "Nunavut." Say it five times fast. Nunavut, nunavut, nunavut, nunavut, nunavut, nunavut. I think that was six times, but it's hard to stop on a dime when you're WASTED.

BIG AL, MARGUERITAVILLE

People are often surprised when they find out that I don't get wasted, I don't even drink. I don't know why everyone assumes that burly people drink, because most of the alcoholics I've ever known looked like skeletons.

I'm not denying that drinking is fun. I especially enjoyed my first time, many years ago at a place on Queen Street called the Cameron House. It was incredible. I was talking to women I normally wouldn't have talked to, I was mouthing off to guys I normally would've feared, I was dancing with everybody, and nobody's opinion mattered to me. This was the night I learned five laws of going out and getting drunk:

1. Do not wear a jacket you cannot afford to lose.

2. Don't worry about money. Someone will always pick up the tab.

3. Nothing you do will embarrass you, provided that you never return to the same bar twice.

4. Do not bring change to the bar or else you will phone somebody and wake them for no reason.

5. There are only two times during a night of drinking: the time you arrive and the time you leave.

What I mean with this last one is that there's a clock at the bar, but you only take notice of it when you arrive and when you leave. Trying to place the time of anything that happened in between is like trying to determine what time you dreamed something.

Stumbling out of the Cameron House at 2 a.m., I was never more helpless while feeling completely bullet-proof. It was about -20°C, but I wasn't cold. I didn't know exactly how I was going to get home, but I didn't care. And for the first time in public, I was truly talking to myself. Not muttering — talking. I was saying things like: "Wow, after all those years of seeing drunks stumbling around on Queen Street, I'm the drunk stumbling around on Queen Street!" and "Hey, I'm talking to myself at full volume, and I can't stop!" and "I'm gonna stop talking to myself right — now. Wait, I'm still doing it!" and "I'd better remember this in case I ever write a book!"

Eventually, I made my way up to Bloor Street and waited for the infamous Bloor night bus. The Toronto transit system shuts down around 2 a.m. except for a handful of "night buses" that run very sporadically on major arteries. The clientele is scary. The Yonge Night Bus is like the ride to a maximum-security prison. And the Bloor night bus is like being in an Iranian maximum-security prison. But something was very different this time. The Bloor night bus felt like home, and all the creeps seemed like long-lost family. One toothless guy covered in tattoos yelled something out the window and then barked at me: "You can't ever take crap from anyone or else you can never be you!" The sober Mike Bullard would have held his breath until getting out at the next stop, taking refuge in the bushes until daylight. The drunk Mike Bullard yelled, "Yeah!" Don't quote me, but I think I also pumped a fist into the air.

When I woke up the next morning, I alternated between throwing up and squirming in pain for about twelve hours. I thought the feeling would never go away. Then I talked to a friend who was an experienced drinker. He told me to eat something and I would feel better. The idea of food disgusted me, but I was willing to try anything. I made some of those McCain pizzas in the toaster-oven and started forcing them down in tiny amounts. It was a pathetic site — I was nibbling like Mahatma Gandhi after a hunger strike. But within minutes, I started to feel normal again. That's when I realized that food is my friend and the bottle is my enemy, and from that day on, I shunned the path of excessive drinking and embraced excessive eating.

Speaking of Gandhi, that is one great movie. Four hours go by like it's four minutes. It sounds like it would be really boring, but it's a fantastic story and Gandhi is laugh-out-loud funny. When they drag him out of prison to meet with the leader of South Africa, the leader offers him food and drink. Gandhi declines with the line: "I dined at the prison." Okay, he's not that funny all the way through, but I'd rank the Mahatma comedically ahead of Robin Williams and Whoopi Goldberg.

The only thing that bothered me about Gandhi in the movie was how he went overboard in using the hunger strike to get his own way. At first it was reasonable: "Until the fighting stops between the Muslims and Hindus, I will not eat." Then they'd report that the fighting had stopped and he'd say: "I need them to French kiss in front of me — then I will eat." They'd actually do it, because nobody can refuse the Mahatma, and then they'd plead with him to eat something. Then he'd say: "When the Academy recognizes the work of Mickey Rooney, then I will eat. Perhaps if I die, Mickey Rooney's bookshelf will finally have to make room for our friend Oscar."

A couple of years later, I hoped for similar magic in a film called *A Passage to India*. Not on your life. Definitely do not rent *A Passage to India* just because *Gandhi* was unavailable. It's like the difference between *Shakespeare in Love*, which was excellent, and an actual work by Shakespeare, which is unbearable.

Hey, Mike: Don't know about you, but I'm sick and tired of psychics claiming they can foresee EVERY-THING about the future. Hope you'll seriously consider having any psychic of your choice on your show and challenge them to predict the exact day my six lottery numbers (or seven numbers if you play Super 7) will come up. My numbers: 2-4-7-12-31-32 and also 33 (with Super 7). Any psychic who can predict (foresee?) the exact day and lottery draw my numbers come up in will receive money from me. If I win $1,000,000 due to their accurate prediction they get $100,000. None of their within a week or even within one or two days difference.

JOHN G., MISSISSAUGA

The psychics don't need your $100,000, because they can just bet on the winning numbers themselves. That's why the wealthiest people in our society are all psychics. Don't be fooled by all those stories about JoJo Savard and people like that filing for bankruptcy; that's just a tax dodge.

Obviously, the psychics are all full of crap (except for Kreskin) and make their living by duping those who are most vulnerable. People approach psychics when they're in dire straits and cling to whatever hope they're given. My favourite psychic was this one who was a guest on a radio phone-in show when I was on tour in Alberta. We couldn't pick up any other radio stations, so I was forced to listen to this fraud for three hours. I got a pretty good sense of how her game works. She gets calls from people who say things like: "I'm worried that my husband is going to leave me." She then says: "He's upset by your intense hatred of cats. You have to change that." The caller says: "I don't have a problem with cats." And here's the way this psychic makes a living: "You do hate cats — you just don't realize it." She was on fire that day, because she managed to point out stuff about all twenty-two callers that the callers themselves did not realize. I wish I could've called to say she's a fraud. When she denied it, I would've said: "You are, but you just don't realize it." I guess I'm a bit of a psychic myself. Oh yeah — quit buying lotto tickets. You've got a better chance of dropping dead right now than you have of winning.

Hey, Mike: Have you ever seen that Dial-A-Date infomercial on late-nite TV? Is that how you met your wife? Why don't you put that annoying guy from the infomercial on your show? Even better, why don't you put me on your show, so I can meet some girls?

CHRIS M., SPRUCE GROVE, ALBERTA

Chris, the annoying Dial-A-Date guy ("Call the number on the screen! The people you're seeing are actual women and men, who you'll talk to when you call the number on the screen!") was on our show during our second week on the air in November 1997. His name is David Bronstein, and he's the only guest to whom I've really been nasty. He didn't do anything wrong on our show, but I have so much distaste for that "dating" scam that I couldn't help myself.

You could argue that it's wrong to invite somebody to be a guest — on your show or in your home — if you're not going to be a gracious host. But our show was only playing on the Comedy Network back then and people weren't lining up to be guests. It's also worth noting that Bronstein expressed a desire to come back, so the experience must've been reasonably pleasant for him. I guess he doesn't get a lot of talk show invitations.

Here is a partial transcript of his appearance on *Open Mike*:

Mike: Well, Dave. What a successful fake life you've had.

DB: Thank you so much for having me, it's a pleasure to be here. I'm very excited.

Mike: Now, how did you get started in this, uh, infomercial deal?

DB: Well, I'm a performer — like you, like Albert [Schultz, the first guest that night].

Mike: Not even close.

DB: Oh, all right, well. This is the David Bronstein roast.

Mike: No, roasts are affectionate. Let's go to a clip of David's show.

(Clip from Dial-A-Date is shown.)

Mike: You know, there's nothing I'd like to do more, Dave, than have you back. But we're just gonna go with fingernails on a chalkboard next time.

DB: You're very funny, Mike. Very funny.

Mike: Well, it's of the moment, really. (Pauses, looks to Stephanie, the floor director.) So, uh, I have no idea what I'm supposed to do next. I'm supposed to keep talking to this guy? Suddenly we're fake. So — you have a wife and two kids —

DB: Beautiful wife. I've been married to the same woman for twelve years.

Mike: Is your wife beautiful?

DB: Beautiful. Beautiful wife. Yes.

Mike: Look, ordinarily I wouldn't do this, but — get out of here.

DB: (to crowd) He's very complimentary, this guy!

Mike: Yeah, well, I'm certainly glad you're mistaking it for flattery. Do we have someone on the phone for David? [For the first couple of months, the show was broadcast live on the Comedy Network and viewers were invited to phone in with questions for the guests.]

Caller: Dave, I wanted to ask you if you knew of any success rate of people meeting one another with your infomercials. [static]

DB: Is there — what?

Mike: The caller wants to know if there's any success due to your big scam. Aside from you and your lovely wife and kids, who are now loaded.

DB: I know somebody — a lady who met a butcher in Hamilton — that's all I know.

Mike: Oh, yeah. And that's the dream, isn't it, folks? A butcher in Hamilton. She could've called him herself for 18 cents a minute, but she pays you $3.99.

DB: $4.99.

Mike: $4.99. Oh, pardon me, Dave. I wouldn't want to upset people. Are you still on the phone, ma'am? (No answer.) Good. I can't believe people call in with questions for this guy. Nobody ever asks questions of me.

DB: See, that's good! I mean, uh, n-not that, not, not (stammers)

Mike: Be quiet! We're going to commercial. We'll be right back.

Oh the early days.

Mike: After watching your show on Friday and seeing you talk with that wacko in the audience I wondered, "What's stopping some weirdo from getting on stage and making a mess of the show?" Orin might stop them but you really should have paid people to take care of drunk/insane members of the audience.

LOVE THE SHOW, BRENDAN THE COMOX IRISHMAN

This is Toronto, Brendan. The drunk and insane are entirely confined to the subway stations.

But if there were to be a disturbance in the middle of our show, I can't see it being a huge problem. We're not exactly *Les Misérables*. There isn't a choreographed song and dance that's going to be ruined. In fact, on most nights we haven't got much of anything planned. Our only hope is that the weirdo who interrupts the show would be different from the one who did it the night before, or else people would think we were paying the guy.

Did I say "the guy"? I'm sorry, you women make fine weirdos, too. By the way, I saw a little of that Women's Television Network recently. I love Jane Hawtin and

She's So Funny, hosted by Mini Holmes, but generally speaking, the Women's Television Network as a concept is a huge stretch. And you can really tell this when they show movies and say things like "We now return to *Superman* — starring Margot Kidder."

The problem is that "women" doesn't say much about what a person will watch on TV. The Golf Channel is for people who watch golf, Country Music Television is for people who like to watch country music stars. Is the Women's Television Network for people who like to look at women? I've seen it, and the answer is definitely no.

It's obviously supposed to cater to women's interests, but women can be interested in anything. Therefore, having a network for women is like having a network for guys named Gene. All the Gene Network could do is say stuff like "We now return to *Superman* ... starring Gene Hackman." For all we know, the Gene Network would outbid Women's Television Network for the rights to *Laverne and Shirley*. Is there any reason guys named Gene wouldn't like *Laverne and Shirley*?

The Women's Television Network has its own version of *Biography* called *Intimate Portrait*, and I'm sure that all women were grateful for that four-part portrait of the life and times of Jaclyn Smith.

Isn't your show in Toronto? Then why the hell is the Saddledome in the background? Who the hell are you trying to fool?

SHAWN B., WEYBURN, SASKATCHEWAN

I guess the jig is up.

Hey, Mike: I live a block away from the Masonic Temple and am very disturbed by the eyesore it has become. Too many lights, too much signage, too many trucks going in and out all day. You are a nuisance!

JT, TORONTO

You can't complain about the lights when you choose to live within a block of Yonge Street. Who doesn't know what Yonge Street represents? I've got an idea: Why don't you move into a house right next to the airport and then complain about the noise?

People like JT are a drag on society. They attack what people are doing without offering any kind of alternative. CTV bought a historic building that otherwise would have been demolished and converted it into something productive. The steep cost had to be offset in part by taking advantage of the advertising potential of the location, which is passed by thousands of people every day. Does JT think there would be no lights or signage if they knocked down the Temple and put up a McDonald's drive-thru?

It's like all those jerks who gripe about toll highways. They just built a toll highway in the Toronto area that runs parallel to the congested Highway 401, and you wouldn't believe the opposition. It was either a toll highway or no highway. The ones who don't want to pay tolls can still take Highway 401, and it's probably less crowded thanks to the arrival of the toll route. Yet I still hear people saying, "The government is sticking it to us, man!" I love how you can automatically become a commoner by adding the word "man" to your sentence. I do it from time to time when I think I'm dealing with someone who might kill me for drug money. I've seen Leno do it when he's interviewing jazz musicians.

Hey, Mike: I'm curious: If you were a kid in 1999, would you sit in your audience and yell stuff out to get attention like all the stupid punks in your audience every night?

LISA T., OWEN SOUND, ONTARIO

If I were a kid in 1999, I'd never leave my house. I'd be afraid of getting swarmed and beaten by any number of those girl gangs. There're guy gangs doing brutal things out there, too, but I feel like I could talk my way out of that, man.

When I was a really young kid, I definitely wouldn't have wanted to be singled out in any audience. Fitting in was crucial. I remember when I was about six years old and I mentioned to a couple of my friends that a football game was "postponed." They let out huge cackles and said "it's not post-poned, it's post-phoned!" The kids all thought the word was pronounced post-phoned. I knew it wasn't. So naturally, I pretended they heard me wrong: "That's what I said, post-phoned." It got them off my back.

When you're really young, you don't know what the hell you're doing. When I was in kindergarten, the teacher told us that the following day was Groundhog Day. She took an afternoon to explain what it was about, and we did something groundhog-related with fingerpaints, which were still toxic in those days. The next morning, when my mom woke me for school, I said, "There's no school — it's Groundhog Day." I thought it was a holiday. She told me I was going anyway, but I screamed: "This is ridiculous! I'm going to be the only one there!" So she let me stay home. I think the reason I was so upset was that going in on a holiday would embarrass me in front of the janitor. I'm not sure that would've been so embarrassing, but I can tell you what was: going in the next day and telling the whole class I stayed home, like everyone else, because of Groundhog Day. That awful moment spawned the hostility you see today.

Another tough day came when I was eight. It was the day I discovered that there are no toys at Grand & Toy. I planned my trip weeks ahead: saved money, obtained bus schedules, etc. I had to take three separate buses to get there. I walked through the entire store about twelve times, because the name of the place made it pretty clear that there were toys somewhere. I eventually asked a clerk, who only took the time to say: "No toys — just office equipment." That's when I decided to make the most of a bad situation. I bought a stapler and played with it for six months.

Hey, Mike! Long-time watcher, first-time writer. I just wanted to say great show! There has been something that I have been wondering about and only you can help me..... I checked out your web page and noticed that you have a brother named Pat. I also noticed that on the show The Love Connection the host's name is Pat Bullard. Any connection? I also noticed that you have the same eyes. Is he your brother? Come on, Mike .... I am on to ya ... let the Canadian viewers know! If he is your brother are there any other famous people in your family? Well, I wish you lots of luck and it's great to see a funny Canadian show.

SERENNA B., TIMMINS, ONTARIO

Well, Serenna, since you brought it up: Yes, Pat Bullard of *The Love Connection* is my younger brother. It's a subject I've never discussed before — except for the twelve thousand times on my show, of which you're a long-time watcher.

Although he's younger, Pat actually preceded me in the comedy business by about eight years. I would supply him with quite a few jokes, but like me, he preferred audience interaction to doing material. By the mid-eighties, he was a rising star in Canada, eventually hosting a short-lived CBC game show, *Baloney*, and his own talk show in Vancouver.

Realizing that a Canadian talk show is a near-impossible proposition because of the lack of star guests, he fled to the U.S. His quick and affable style made him a popular choice to warm up sitcom audiences in L.A., and before long he was writing and producing for *Roseanne* and *Grace Under Fire*. But all along he worked behind the scenes to fulfil his dream of being a talk show host, and in the fall of 1996 he got his chance from a syndicator called Multimedia, which was responsible for the Phil Donahue and Jerry Springer shows.

At that time, all the daytime talk shows were sleaze-fests, and Pat had this idea that he would focus on light celebrity interviews in the spirit of the old Mike Douglas and Merv Griffin shows. But a few months before his debut, Rosie O'Donnell's show hit the airwaves. Rosie was a smash, proving that Pat had the right idea, but by the time Pat got on the air, there were already several new and established shows going the same route. Besides, it's almost impossible for a new show to make it in day-time. Out of seventeen new daytime talk shows launched the previous year — hosted by people like Carnie Wilson, Tempestt Bledsoe, Gabrielle Carteris, and Danny Bonaduce — only one made it to a second season (*The Gordon Elliot Show*).

In other words, it's no reflection on my brother that *The Pat Bullard Show* lasted only about six months. It went off the air without fanfare, except for a nasty shot from David Spade on his *Saturday Night Live* feature, "The Hollywood Minute." Spade announced Pat's cancellation, and then said that the show "made me yearn for the sharp bite of *Mike and Maty*" (an extremely fluffy show cancelled the year before by ABC). He then mumbled something to "Weekend Update" anchor Norm Macdonald.

Anyway, Pat's show ended and he went on to host a revival of *The Love Connection*. Although Pat never set out to be a game show host, it was worth doing because he'd been promised that the show would give him a chance to demonstrate his ad lib skills. It's worth remembering that Johnny Carson first came to North America's attention as a game show host. Unfortunately, most of Pat's ad libs were edited from the show by a producer who thought comedy should take a back seat to romantic intrigue. Good call.

Being the host of *The Love Connection* is not a bad thing. It might not make it easier to go to your high-school reunion, but it pays huge money for about forty days' work. Pat's very overqualified to be doing that sort of thing, but it's going to be very hard for him to live the talk show dream because he's not a hideous freak.

We're used to them now, but Jay Leno, David Letterman, and Conan O'Brien all look like they grew up too close to a nuclear plant. Pat is classically handsome. The same great looks that have helped make him the centre of attention at every social function he's ever attended have hindered him in the comedy field, because people don't want to accept that anyone can have it all. The public is prepared to accept people who are exceptionally attractive and other people who are exceptionally funny. But they will not accept people who are both.

I noticed a great example of this phenomenon on *The*

Tonight Show. Kathie Lee Gifford was the guest. She looked very good, and Leno said so. Then when she attempted to be funny, the crowd froze her out. About a year later, I saw her on the show again, only this time she was the second guest. The first guest was Farrah Fawcett. Next to Farrah, Kathie Lee looked barely dateable, and this time she got enormous laughs.

When a great-looking guy gets on stage at a comedy club, he's already got two strikes against him. His best bet at that point is to do something self-deprecating, but leading-man types have a hard time coming up with credible jokes along those lines. They can hire mutants like me to write something for them, but that just sticks in their craw. The fact that Pat has gone as far as he has despite his good looks is a testament to just how incredibly funny he is.

Although a variety of factors, including a lot of luck, converged to make me a Canadian talk show success, I know it couldn't have happened without my scruffy, bald, and overweight appearance. If Pat was the host of our show, the Canadian public would've taken one look at him and said, "If this guy's so good, what the hell is he still doing in Canada?" Instead they saw me and said, "We'd better support this guy, because they don't hire misfits like that in Hollywood."

Our show actually benefited from Pat's U.S. talk show in a variety of ways. My producer, Al Magee, got his first TV experience working on Pat's show. So did Sean Tweedley, who produces our remote pieces and is best known to viewers as "The Walk-on Guy" and the "Mid-show Review Guy." But most importantly, Pat taught me that you've got to err on the side of good manners with guests — "hug 'em before you slug 'em" — and that a twinkle in your eye and a smile go a long way towards making whatever comes out of your mouth extremely palatable. Comedy club-goers may recall my persona in those days as basically stone-faced, which was fine then, because nobody had a clicker in their hand and I had forty-five minutes to show everyone my true colours. On TV, where you can be turned off at any time and the camera exaggerates all of your facial expressions, a nasty countenance can impart a mean-spiritedness to your jokes that's not really there.

Pat hasn't appeared on a regular edition of *Open Mike*, but he was a guest on our live New Year's Eve special on December 31, 1998. It was a very strange situation, but not for the reasons everyone thought. People thought that I was tense because I was afraid Pat would steal the spotlight and upstage me like he's done throughout our lives. People thought Pat would be tense because he always wanted a talk show like mine and there was my face on the side of a Yonge Street landmark. There wasn't much truth to either proposition.

What made it strange for me was that CTV sunk a ton of money into this New Year's Eve special, and I couldn't figure out why anyone would want to watch me talk to my brother. I was thinking: I've known this guy all my life, I've threatened to tell on him for a million different things over the course of his life — I have told on him for a million different things — what could possibly make this good television for the people at home? That was the thing that freaked me out.

As for the concept of two comedians trying to out-zing one another, we'd been doing that at the kitchen table for twenty years. Who knew it was suddenly of interest to the general public? I only realized after the fact that people were watching that segment with a scorecard to keep track of who was getting in the most jabs. I think it was a draw, but you can be the judge. Here's a transcript, picking up just after I mistakenly tried to throw to a commercial.

Mike: My next guest has hosted two of his own talk shows, written for *Grace Under Fire* and *Roseanne*, and is currently the star of *The Love Connection*. I'll never forget the first time I saw him ... he was naked, crying, and stealing all my mother's affection. Not much has changed. Please welcome Pat Bullard.

Pat enters.

Mike: Great to see you.

Pat: How exciting.

Mike: Isn't it wonderful?

Pat: My god, is it time for a commercial? You run this like a well-oiled machine, don't you?

Mike: As a matter of fact, if this continues, we'll go right to commercial.

Pat: I apologize, I thought we were at home. Orin, my man!

Orin: Pat, what you sayin'?

Pat: All right, with the get down ... (unintelligible jive talk). Orin, happy Lufthansa, I wanted to say that. I know that's an important holiday to you and your people. I haven't seen Orin since Sean from the show got married and Orin stayed at my house. We had a good time, didn't we?

Orin: You got a fat crib, baby. You're *livin'*. You're livin' in L.A., boy.

Pat: Haven't got a clue what you said, Orin. Thanks, though. Orin stayed, and he stayed a couple of extra days, and to be honest with you, there's stuff missing. Ah, we're havin' a good time, aren't we, Orin? Seriously, Orin, there's a blue vase. If that's in my dressing room after the show, then all is forgiven. (To first guest, Tom Cochrane) Tom, a suit and a tie, would it have killed you? (To Mike) It's a fun year. When do *you* talk? (Huge applause.)

Mike: Y'know, I'm really sorry. I didn't want to interrupt your flashback to hosting. (Huge applause.) So, what did you think of 1998, Pat?

Pat: It was a good year, Mike. *I* enjoyed it. This is so stupid. (To Tom) Do you have a brother?

Tom: No, two sisters.

Pat: Well, don't ever let them interview you. Boy, what a year, Mike.

Mike: Yeah, I bet. How's the family?

Pat: This is like the dinner table. I just wanna punch you in the head.

Mike takes a hard swat at Pat to the delight of the crowd.

Tom: This is turning into Jerry Springer.

Pat: It *is* a little Springer.

Mike: Beautiful tux. It used to be mine. Still getting hand-me-downs?

Pat: Yeah, *you* were this size once, Mike. (Huge applause.)

Mike: What better time to say, how's *The Love Connection* going?

Pat: *Love Connection*'s doing well. Dad was joking backstage and he said this was broadcast.

Mike: Yeah, let's see how you're doing with our audience — how they voted. I'm sorry.

Pat: No, that's okay.

Mike: How could I forget. It's the same line that's repeated every night. Night after night after night.

Pat: Not that you've ever repeated a joke. (Imitating Mike) Oh, what a tangled web we weave. You know what? I was backstage reading *People* magazine and they had an interview with George Michael after that whole [arrest] thing. George Michael said that he didn't think he was gay until he was twenty-nine years old. Apparently he never saw the *Wake Me Up Before You Go-Go* video.

Mike: May I say right now that I've always enjoyed that one.

Pat: (To audience) He doesn't even know who George is — he's got one Barbra Streisand album. That's all he has in his whole collection.

Mike: And there's absolutely nothing wrong with that. I believe she's big. Now, have you had weird couples on the show?

Pat: Yeah. It's fun, actually. I wasn't sure whether I'd enjoy the show, but we have people on — we had a couple on — this is when you know you're getting old — I had a couple on, they had met for their date, and five minutes into it she recommended they go hiking naked in the woods. And this is how I know I'm getting old, 'cause I thought: *Hiking*? Jesus Christ, woman, why don't we go to the gym?

Mike: We don't say that up here.

Pat: My favourite thing I read this morning — it was in the *Sun* — it was about a guy in Edmonton who killed his wife and the insurance company refused to pay him because he didn't tell them he was gonna kill his wife. How the hell would that work? You're gettin' a big policy: "Listen, by the way, I'm probably gonna kill my wife." "Get outta here, you knucklehead, we're writin' you a cheque!"

Mike: We can plant some heavy laughter in there during post-production. Now, you worked for both Brett Butler and Roseanne —

Pat: It's not like you haven't had practice, I'm sure. You, my friend — and I shouldn't brag about my own brother — you, my friend, are the new Jack Duffy. (Big laugh and applause.)

Mike: (Looking at interview card) And, uh —

Pat: Boy, you can sure hide that reading thing.

Mike: I was just double-checking. (Pointing at card) Yes, there it is, "You are the new Jack Duffy." (Applause.) All right, let's drop this and go to mutual admiration for the last ten seconds. I'm very proud of you.

Pat: Thank you, I'm proud of you. I think this is a fantastic setup. (Huge applause.)

Dear Mike: Do you remember your first time on stage? Where was it? Were you always an ad libber or did your do prepared jokes? If there's any videotape of the evening, I'd kill to see it.

MELISSA, KENTVILLE, NOVA SCOTIA

If there was videotape, you would *have* to kill to see it. Even when it goes well, a comedian's first time on stage is embarrassingly awkward in retrospect. There's almost nothing in that first performance that a comedian would still be doing five years later.

My first time was in 1986 at the original Yuk Yuk's club in Toronto, which closed in 1994 — some would say there's a connection, but that's ridiculous. My brother had been a comedian for six years and, now a rising star, was about to move to Vancouver. I thought there might be an opportunity to establish my own identity, and my friend and current producer Al Magee pushed me extremely hard to give it a try. He told me that if I didn't do it then, I'd never do it and always regret it. I thought he was acting altruistically but, obviously, he was just envisioning a job for himself down the road. And he really knew what he was doing because, on that fateful first night in 1986, a scout from CTV saw me and offered me a talk show for the 1997 season.

Pat's celebrity in the stand-up community meant there was quite a bit of pressure on me that first night. I didn't have the anonymity you really need to relax up there. Every Yuk Yuk's headline act was at the back of the room to see how Pat's big brother would do. Pat was extremely encouraging, even though it could have been humiliating for him as well as for me. I considered using a pseudonym for both our sakes, but then I realized that I'm the eldest and, if anyone was going to change their name, it should be him.

Incidentally, many of these headline acts who seemed so intimidating back then are fringe talents who live in their car today. But when you're starting out they seem godlike just by virtue of the fact that they do comedy for a *living*. To a guy who installs phones, that looks mighty impressive. Furthermore, they could easily do forty-five minutes on stage while I was hoping to survive for five.

The MC that night was veteran Yuk Yuk's comedian Larry Horowitz, who gave me this gem of an introduction: "I don't know a lot about this guy, but his brother's a headliner here — please welcome Mike Bullard." Those words always stayed in my head, especially when I became a top MC and was introducing other comedians. Sometimes when I'd drive to gigs with Horowitz, I'd have flashbacks and want to pummel him. But I never confronted him about it, because I knew it'd hurt him more if I put it in this book.

Like any amateur with any hope of success, I began my comedic odyssey with prepared material. No matter how quick and entertaining you are while just screwing around with your friends, it's suicide to try to ad lib your way through your first time on stage. Every week, people who are funny at parties are chewed up and spat out at amateur nights across the country because they didn't anticipate the pressure of facing an audience that expects immediate results. And you can't produce those results when you're too busy adjusting to the light in your face and the echo of your own voice bouncing off the back wall. The guys who make the mistake of winging it on amateur night, and it is ninety-five percent guys, rarely return for a second performance.

I know you're curious what kind of jokes I did that first night. I'll tell you, but you have to believe me when I say they're probably no more embarrassing than the ones Jerry Seinfeld did on his first night.

"Do Inuit cops feel foolish when they yell 'freeze'?"

I didn't expect to kill with this stuff. In fact, I was terrified to go on stage. I didn't really believe I had what it took, and just thought, Okay, good, I'll finally get it over with, bomb, and my wife and my best friend will get off my back and tell me I was right and they were wrong.

Somehow, I got huge laughs that night. And as far as I'm concerned, that evening screwed me out of a Bell Canada vice-presidency.

I didn't start improvising on stage for another four months. That was around the time the club promoted me to Friday and Saturday nights, which was great because audiences are exponentially better the more they pay to get in. For example, when I started on amateur night, it was sponsored by local radio station CKFM 99.9, so it cost ninety-nine cents to get in. Later, when it was taken over by Q107 and cost $1.07, we got more of the class of people you want in an audience.

I still remember the pivotal moment that took me from reciting material to ad libbing. A woman in the audience said, "If you had bigger eyes, you'd look like Kenny Rogers." I said "If you had decent breasts, you'd look like Dolly Parton." That was my first ad lib and I'll never forget it. The crowd went nuts, and that's when I learned that it's very hard to follow up good ad libbing with a prepared act. I would've been better off that night if I hadn't made that quick comeback, because it made the rest of my material seem really dull.

I wanted to expand to all ad libbing, but Yuk Yuk's wouldn't allow it from an unseasoned act. Company policy. I persisted with my request, and ended up exiled from Yuk Yuk's for almost 2 years, until Evan Adelman joined the company as a talent booker and embraced my comedy style. Before long, I was hosting shows at Yuk Yuk's clubs all over southern Ontario while continuing to work for Bell Canada during the day.

From that point, it took several years to hone my ad libbing to the level it's at now. The best approach varies from comic to comic but, for me, the most important thing I learned was to listen to the crowd and roll with the punches rather than anticipate. I don't even clear my head when I go up there. I figure there are four spotlights on me, I've waited for this all my life, I have a microphone in front of me. Now is my opportunity to manipulate three hundred people into coming around to my point of view and thinking I'm funny. That's all I ever think when going on stage.

In the early days I had a few lines I'd use every night. Once, this guy told me he's a printer for a living, so I said, "You'll move on to writing eventually." It got a huge laugh, so after that I'd scan the crowd before the show for people with ink under their fingernails. Then I'd ask them what they do, and they almost always said they were printers. Then I'd hit them with the line. But one day, I happened upon a guy whose fingers were blue because they had been slammed in a car door. He said he's a courier, so I said, "You'll move on to writing eventually." That kind of backfired, and also offended every courier in the room. That was the best thing that could've happened. After that, I never planned anything before going on stage. Going in unprepared is the best approach for me comedically. The fact that it's also incredibly lazy is a complete coincidence.

Hey, Mike: You're always making fun of Newfoundland when it's really Toronto that sucks. Please read this on the air.

TOM R.

Okay, Tom, but you're obviously unaware that, unlike Newfoundland and every other whiny region in Canada, Toronto doesn't care about being criticized — unless the criticism comes from the United States. That's when we build domed stadiums and stage blockbuster musicals, hoping the Americans will notice.

Vancouver and Montreal are hurt when they think they've been insulted by Toronto, but these insults don't really exist. Toronto doesn't think long enough about the rest of Canada to even form an opinion about it. I'm sure Calgarians have some kind of take on Vancouver and Montreal, but Vancouver and Montreal wouldn't care, just like Calgary wouldn't be troubled by a hate letter from Medicine Hat. There's a whole food chain, and Newfoundland has to be at or near the bottom of it. I can't think of any part of the country that would get offended by criticism from Newfoundland, but I don't know much about Labrador. Who knows, maybe Newfoundland looks like Emerald City when you live in Labrador.

The reality is, people are more or less the same everywhere. As a comedian who does a nightly monologue, I depend heavily on whatever geographical stereotypes are well known, whether or not there's a grain of truth behind them. Without preconceived notions, there can be very few jokes in the world. The best comedy comes from universal truths, but there aren't nearly enough of those to fill five shows a week. If people across the country believe that Toronto is a crime-infested hell-hole, even though it has a crime rate lower than virtually every other city in Canada, then as a comedian I'm happy to go along with that.

Here, then, is the comedian's guide to Canada:

British Columbia

A rainy colony of Starbucks outlets where the laid-back people are all addicted to heroin.

Alberta

Where gun-crazed calf-ropers constantly re-elect a premier who demolishes hospitals in between drinking binges.

Saskatchewan

Nothing but farmers ploughing their totally flat land. Good for no more than two jokes a year.

Manitoba

Home of Winnipeg, where it's really cold ten months per year. The other two months, it doesn't exist.

Ontario

Toronto: squeegee kids, crazy mayor, dirty and dangerous subways, full of itself.

Hamilton: armpit of the country.

Niagara Falls: tacky rip-off (true).

Ottawa: senators always absent.

Northern ninety percent of province: doesn't exist.

Quebec

Chain-smoking, English-hating separatists who have sex with really young girls (men) or really old men (Celine Dion).

Maritimes

That's right, we make no distinction between Nova Scotia, New Brunswick, and P.E.I. In fact, we rarely make reference to them at all, but if a news story forces us to, we pretend that they're all fishermen. For example: "In Moncton, N.B., a world record was set when local children gathered over two thousand Easter eggs — Unfortunately, the Easter egg stocks are now depleted and there can be no more hunts for at least ten years." To the best of my knowledge, there was never any fishing in Moncton. But I bet you laughed.

Newfoundland

Still the mother lode. If we had to pay royalties to Newfoundland for every joke made at its expense, it would no longer be the poorest province. In fact, that's how I view the tax money we funnel into Newfoundland year after year: comedy royalties. So let's stop calling them transfer payments. In fact, I look forward to the day when we routinely talk about how Newfies spend all of their comedy royalties on booze.

Yukon, Northwest Territories, Nunavut

The bread basket of the country, once global warming reaches its peak in about twenty years. For now, it doesn't exist.

Hey, Mike: Why did Mike Bullard treat Preston (Hitler) Manning with such kid gloves? Why not just help every white, racist, fascist, religious zealot in the country while you're at it? Do you even realize that his father, E.C. Manning, once supported the censorship of the media in Alberta?

Like, what's next ... are you gonna invite the Ku Klux Klan on, too?

ANONYMOUS

We wanted to do a comedic reply to this on the air by saying, "You obviously didn't see our show on January 15. Here's a clip." We'd then cut to me wrapping up the show: "My thanks to Melanie Doane — you can pick up her new CD at HMV, Bruce Gray is on *Traders* on Global on Thursday nights at 10, and the Grand Wizard will be burning crosses near Orillia all this weekend — check out his Web site for details. And I'm on the Comedy Network and CTV — Goodnight!" Then we'd see all the guests, including the white-hooded KKK guy, shaking hands and dancing while the band plays the closing theme.

However, our producer, Al Magee, rightly pointed out that we shouldn't imply that we condone an e-mail comparing a legitimate party leader to white supremacists. These comparisons are not only insulting to Preston Manning and the thousands of Albertans who voted for him, but are also an irresponsible trivializing of the evils of the Klan and Hitler. It's also idiotic to support the comparison by pointing out something Manning's *father* once did, and also to equate the word "white" with the words "fascist," "racist," and "zealot."

Frankly, it's impressive that this e-mailer managed to cram so much ignorance into just eight lines.

Hey, Mike: I have watched your show since it started. Sometimes it is good, sometimes not ... and sometimes GREAT. But tonight, I watched and heard your announcement that you were not going to do any more Balkan War jokes. I am not sure yet if I agree that Canada has done the right thing, but I absolutely agree that no matter what side you are on, it is not a joking matter and I admire your professional courage in making the statement that you did. I will still be a loyal fan and watch the show but you just went up a bunch of points in my ratings scale.

REGARDS,
PETER B., MOSER RIVER, NOVA SCOTIA.

Can you figure out why I made a point of putting this e-mail in the book? I think you can.

That's right, it's the only e-mail we've received in two years that doesn't have a spelling mistake. We keep the original under lock and key.

On March 31, about a week after NATO began bombing Yugoslavia, I took a moment at the end of the show to announce that I wouldn't do any more jokes pertaining to the war because the depth of the ethnic cleansing tragedy was too grave. I had seen Kosovars packed into trains like the Jews going to death camps, and it drove home how inappropriate it would be to make light of the situation.

Thus began the real war: the one between me and my writers. They made the following points:

1. Every other talk show on television was doing jokes about the war. We were putting ourselves at a competitive disadvantage. When O.J. Simpson was charged with murder in 1994, David Letterman refused to do any jokes about it. Asked why, he simply said that there's nothing funny about double homicide. After three months, he changed his policy and did all kinds of O.J. material because Leno was clobbering him in the ratings with the Dancing Itos and stuff like that. Apparently there can be something funny about double homicide. When you get right down to it, Letterman made the mistake of ignoring what was on everybody's mind at the time — a fatal error for a show that does topical material. People always talk about Letterman's Oscar hosting and Leno's Hugh Grant interview as the events that turned the ratings tide in Leno's favour, but it was more likely Leno's monopoly on the O.J. issue.

2. Fundamentally, what's the difference between doing jokes about Saddam Hussein and Slobodan Milosovic? Both engaged in ethnic slaughter, yet we never think twice about doing Saddam Hussein jokes. Letterman took this big moral stand about "double homicide," but he had done all kinds of material on Jeffrey Dahmer and the Unabomber. It's hypocrisy.

3. They did Hitler jokes during the Second World War. Bob Hope's NBC radio show took shots at the Führer all the time. How can we be more conservative than *Bob Hope*?

4. Just because the packed trains evoked images of the Holocaust, it doesn't mean that's what was happening. Those trains weren't going to death camps. They were going across the border where relief workers were waiting. Not a happy experience, to be sure, but not Auschwitz either.

5. It's not intrinsically wrong to do humour on serious subjects, as long as the jokes don't target the victims. Drunk driving is a serious subject, but nobody would think twice about doing a Ted Kennedy joke. The jokes we had been doing on the war were working because they weren't remotely about the refugees. For example, when local Serbs fire-bombed the U.S. consulate in Toronto just before a weekend, we began a monologue by saying, "This just in — for those of you planning your weekend activities — the annual open house at the U.S. consulate has been cancelled." What on earth is offensive about that? The following week, when Serbs protested at the McDonald's in Belgrade, the writers wrote jokes like: "They refrained from fire-bombs this time, fearing that the grease fire would destroy the city." They added that "the violent mob dispersed when one of the McDonald's employees threatened to call the manager." Pretty tame. But this was after the ban on war material, so the jokes weren't even considered. This was the same week that Bill Maher scored a huge ovation by saying that the Serbs declared an Easter cease-fire because "they needed the time to do some spring cleansing."

6. Viewer comments like the one in the above e-mail tend to be insincere. There's not one person on earth who claimed to be interested in O.J. Simpson or Monica Lewinsky, but talk shows that veered away from those topics when they were hot were annihilated in the ratings. If the war takes over the news for a year, how long will it be before every viewer in Canada — including this e-mailer — starts tuning in to Craig Kilborn to see what outrageous comments he makes? Keep in mind, even people who *hate* Don Cherry watch him. People who hate me continue to watch.

7. Are we really honouring our brave men and women overseas when we ignore the war? Would they be happy to know that, while they're over there hungry and bleeding, we're pretending that the war's not even happening? If the war is so damn serious, it's sort of offensive to act as if the biggest thing in the news is a seagull hitting Fabio's face.

So, that's what the writers threw at me day after day. Despite that, I'm staying out of it. It just doesn't feel right and when it comes down to it, the country doesn't watch the writers. They watch me. And I'm not comfortable with doing that kind of material.

My position on this remains firm, and I can explain why in two words: "Uncle Slobodan."

Generally speaking, our show goes out of its way to err on the side of good taste. Would you expect anything else from Canada's talk show? It drives our writers nuts to see good jokes thrown away — jokes that almost certainly would make the cut on the American shows. But my producers and I get the feeling that our viewers have a different expectation than those of the American shows. Otherwise, they'd be watching those shows instead of us. Besides, I only do five or six written jokes a night, while people like Jay Leno and Craig Kilborn do twenty-five to thirty, so I can afford to be selective.

Al Magee and I have to make decisions on material every day. Sometimes as a matter of taste, sometimes because of timing, we don't always get to do jokes that we think are very funny. Now, for purely educational purposes, here's a list of rejected *Open Mike* monologue jokes never before seen by the public — except for the other people who paid for the right to know everything about the show when they bought this book.

Newfoundland is celebrating its fiftieth anniversary in Canada tonight. The federal government is paying for a big party — which basically sums up the fifty years.
Too cruel on their birthday.

The leader of the Ontario Green Party said he'll be campaigning on a bicycle to bring attention to the need for better accommodation for cyclists on our roads. And his point was especially well made today, when he was run over by the Tory campaign bus.
Image of a guy getting run over.

A player on the New York Knicks has filed a complaint about female reporters in the locker room. Let me guess — it's the only white guy on the team.
Stereotyping.

NATO bombers hit Serbian television studios with a cruise missile yesterday. But they were back on the air just hours after the bombing, breaking the old record set by Ralph Benmergui.
No Kosovo jokes; reluctant to slam fellow Canadian host.

The *Howie Mandel Show* was officially cancelled today. Which is too bad, but he had it coming. I mean, have you seen the show? He comes on at the beginning, talks to audience members — that kind of crap's never gonna fly.
Disrespectful to fellow host.

A big summit on homelessness begins in Toronto tomorrow. Jean Chrétien can't make it, but plans to phone in from one of his five houses.
Nobody followed the Chrétien residence scandal.

In Japan, a former employee of Bridgestone Tires walked into a board meeting, stripped down, and slashed his stomach in an attempt to commit hara-kiri. Luckily, a quick-thinking co-worker sealed the wound with Tire-in-a-Can spray.
Violent imagery.

The Good Humor ice cream company is closing its plant in Montreal. Yeah, Good Humor was a tough sell in Quebec. It'll be replaced by "Physical Humor."
Only comedy pros will get it.

The mayor of St. John's, Newfoundland, is refusing to give the key to the city to the premier of China because of human rights abuses. The mayor said he can't condone a regime under which the living conditions are so bad that huge numbers of people leave for a better life.
Too cruel to a whole region of viewers.

Tory MP David Price stood up in Parliament yesterday and charged that Canadian commandos are engaged in a top-secret mission inside Kosovo. Defence minister Art Eggleton denied that, saying, "It's not a secret any more, jerk." This Price guy is out of control: Today he got up in the House and read out the unlisted phone numbers and addresses of attractive single women who live alone.
Kosovo.

Don Cherry says Wayne Gretzky made a mistake in retiring at this point. And Gretzky should listen, because Cherry managed his NHL career perfectly — he hung on as long as he could, knowing he might regret it if he didn't stay for the whole game.
People don't know about Cherry's one-game playing career.

Basketball star Scottie Pippen was pulled over last night and charged with drunk driving. Finally, a story about a professional athlete who's not soliciting a prostitute.
Too flip about drunk driving.

Pippen drunk driving — I guess he picked a bad night to have a triple-double.
I didn't get it.

In fairness to Pippen, it was pretty hard walking a straight line with all of those opposing fans hooting and waving stuff to distract him.
I didn't get it.

In a related story, another former Chicago Bull, Dennis Rodman, can't get arrested.
Not funny enough.

Slobodan Milosevic yesterday called CNN a "house of lies." Although, I only heard about it on CNN, so maybe he never really said it.
Kosovo.

A New York doctor is marketing a TV powered by a bicycle to force couch potatoes to exercise while watching. And for those of you who want to watch adult pay-per-view movies, there's also a rowing machine version.
I should have done this one.

Yes, the Great One has called it quits. I guess that explains all the weeping at the Albanian border today.
Kosovo; disrespectful to Gretzky.

Yesterday, the prime minister unveiled a stamp commemorating one hundred years of the Sikh religion in Canada. The prime minister also lifted a ban on Sikh students attending class while wearing their ceremonial letter-openers.
Would offend Sikhs.

Wayne Gretzky said yesterday that it would take a miracle for him to come back next season. Yeah, like him scoring another goal.
Attacking a national hero.

The Ottawa Senators were bounced from the playoffs yesterday. Captain Alexei Yashin was criticized for not contributing a single point in the series. But you knew he wouldn't show up — he's a Senator.
Hackneyed reference to senators' attendance record.

Air Canada has formed a new business alliance with Mexican airline Mexicana de Aviacion. Air Canada sees this as an opportunity to do more business in Mexico. In fact, they've already launched a new slogan: "Sneak in from the North."

Offensive to Hispanics.

In the U.S. on Friday, a new beer was launched that caters specifically to the homosexual community. It's called Gay Pride Beer. Great — just when bar slap fights were on the decline.

Offensive to gays.

Defence Minister Art Eggleton says our armed forces are running out of money because of the Kosovo crisis. Which explains the long lineup of Canadian troops outside the Albanian Money Mart.

Kosovo.

Actress Delta Burke will be going on a cross-Canada tour to promote her new line of plus-size clothes for Zellers. Monica Lewinsky, if you're out there: Peer into the future. This is you in twenty years. Enjoy the red-carpet treatment while you can.

Offensive to the overweight; not that funny.

Five thousand Kosovar refugees have begun moving into Canadian military bases. The government is promising to thoroughly screen them to weed out known terrorists, who will then be relocated to mansions in Toronto and Vancouver.

Kosovo.

As you may have heard, Ontario lakes and rivers are drying up because of environmental change. But Tourism Ontario wants you to know that we're still open for business, and invites you to ride on Niagara Falls' new tour boat: *Maid of the Trickle. Baywatch* should relocate here. That way, when someone needs to be rescued in the water, that sexy sprint could go for three quarters of a mile.

Not funny enough.

The Senate is voting on a new extradition bill that would make it easier to send our criminals to other countries. It's also hoped that such legislation will make it easier to get other countries to send our senators back here.

I never find these Senate jokes funny.

At the World Hockey Championships in Norway today, Canada beat Italy 5–2. But it was a competitive game. I heard the Italian goalie put up a brick wall. Then they made him take it down.

Offensive to Italians.

The city of Mississauga says that if it's unable to relocate 1500 Canadian geese, it'll have no choice but to kill them. Maybe so, but did they have to announce that the same week 1500 Kosovar refugees are arriving? This won't put them at ease.

Kosovo.

Nelson Mandela said yesterday that he has done his duty for South Africa and plans to retire into obscurity. You know what that means — he's hosting an improv show on the Comedy Network.

Disloyal to my employer.

The Serbs and the Chinese protested together on Parliament Hill yesterday. Boy, Serbia and China: talk about your moral authorities. If they can get the Libyans and Iranians involved, we'll have to take notice.

Too political.

Newfoundland nurses are striking. They want more hours and less pay.

I was saving this one for the book.

DESK BITS AND BITES

For the hardcore fans and wannabe comedians, a selection of desk bits from the show.

Eerie Similarities

A comparison of two topical entities that have startlingly common characteristics. Such as Calista Flockhart and a bucket of KFC. Consistently our most comedically effective desk bit.

1. **Kenneth Starr and Bill Clinton**
   Both of their careers hinge on Monica Lewinsky.
   Both haven't had enough sex.
   Both would like to see Hillary behind bars.

2. **Mark McGwire and Elizabeth Taylor**
   Both have back problems.
   Both reached their late sixties because of drugs.
   Both have surpassed records previously held by Babe Ruth (McGwire for home runs; Taylor for eating hot dogs).

3. **Shania Twain and famed sumo wrestler Akebono**
   The love of Shania's life, a 200lb guy named "Mutt."
   The love of Akebono's life, 200lbs of mutton.
   Shania is one-eighth Ojibway.
   Akebono once ate an Ojibway.
   Both have difficulty finding shirts that cover their entire stomach.

4. The Royal Family and a twenty-five-year-old door mat

Both have worn out their "Welcome."

5. Sasquatch and the movie *The Avengers*

Both apparently stink awfully badly.

Both have been seen by only a handful of people.

6. David Foster and alcohol

Both have almost killed Ben Vereen.

7. Barbershop quartets and the federal Tory party

Both are groups made up of people who sing the same tune.

Both have about four members.

8. Bill Clinton and JFK

Both Democrats.

Both elected at a young age.

Both ended their presidency by staining a dress.

9. The Backstreet Boys and a giant meteor headed towards Earth

Both cause panic in the streets.

Both are made up of dense material.

Both must be stopped.

10. Monica Lewinsky and a vacuum cleaner

Both are handy around the office.

Both have been used by Ken Starr in a zealous attempt to pick up dirt.

Both have been represented by William Ginsburg.

Clinton prefers both to Hillary.

11. Charles Barkley and Fred Flintstone

Both are insufferable loud-mouths.

Both have enormous feet.

Both are furious over being locked out.

12. Doug Flutie and Rusty from *The Friendly Giant*

Both wasted their most productive years in Canada.

Both are known for scrambling.

Both have been sacked by giants.

13. Alberta and Russia

Both are plagued by power failures.

Neither can afford to keep their good hockey players.

Both have burly leaders who are drunk by 9 a.m.

14. Calista Flockhart and a bucket of Kentucky Fried Chicken

Both are all neck and legs.

Both claim to be healthy.

Both weigh about six pounds.

15. Lucien Bouchard and Roger Clemens

Both are married to American women.

Both are responsible for a lot of strikes.

Both will pretend to negotiate before bolting from Canada.

16. Tommy Lee and Tommy Lee Jones

Both are named Tommy Lee.

Both have spent time around fugitives.

Tommy Lee Jones has been thrown from a horse;
Tommy Lee is hung like a horse.

17. Your grandfather and the Oscars

Both are in their seventies.

Both seem to go on and on.

Both are obsessed with the Second World War.

You only see them once a year.

18. College basketball players and the recently striking school janitors in Toronto

Both have seen sweat mopped off the floor.

Both are familiar with keys.

Both have been around the rim.

Neither can afford to travel.

Both don't spend much time in the classroom.

Most won't make it to the NBA.

19. KISS guitarist Paul Stanley as the Phantom of the Opera and the Canadian women's hockey team

Both have been slammed by purists.

Both have kicked k.d. lang out of their dressing room.

Both wear make-up behind a mask.

20. Fans at the Lewis-Holyfield fight and your dad on Christmas morning

Both are drunk.

Both are disappointed with a tie.

Both vowed never to do this again.

Both are witness to a one-sided beating.

Both blame a woman for the judging.

21. **St. Patrick's Day revellers and workers at the Pickering nuclear plant**

Both rely on luck.

Both have a complete disregard for safety.

Both have a green hue.

Both show up anticipating an accident.

22. **Lennox Lewis and Jacques Parizeau**

Both have squeezed a lot of money out of the English.

Both have blamed their losses on foreigners.

Both go the full twelve rounds before staggering home.

23. **The Montreal Canadiens and fermenting grapes**

Both stink.

Both get stomped.

Both are obsessed over by the French.

Both will end up in the cellar.

24. **Striking CBC workers and the Montreal Expos**

No one pays attention to their strikes.

No one will notice when they're gone.

Both refuse to go inside their buildings.

Government refuses to fund either.

Both worried someone will steal their signs.

25. **The United States prison population and Vancouver**

Both total around two million.

Both cut off from the real world.

Both on drugs.

Both get about an hour of sunlight a day.

26. Tim Johnson and Bill Clinton

Neither went to Vietnam.

Both lost credibility because of lying.

Both known for commanding the BJs.

(If you know what I mean).

27. Tyson/Botha fight and the desk chat between me and Orin

Both feature two stocky guys not in the best shape of their lives, engaging in awkward, flailing exchanges ....

One getting paid more than the other.

28. Y2K and Newfoundland

Both could deplete all of our assets.

Both make you think it's 1900.

Both too late to fix.

29. Toronto Mayor Mel Lastman and a minivan

Both are compact.

Both are kind of embarassing.

Neither can handle the snow.

30. Hillary Clinton and Pope John Paul II

Both are forgiving.

Both probably prefer to wear pants.

Both abstained their way to the top.

31. Pavel Bure and Fidel Castro

Both associated with Russian Rockets.

Both have sent people scurrying to Miami.

Both find Mike Keenan overbearing.

32. Mike and the *Titanic*

Both bulky and monstrous.

Both have victims buried in Halifax.

Interest in both peaked in 1998.

Neither made it to America.

33. The Olympics and the circus

Both will bring rings to your town in exchange for hookers.

Both feature bearded women.

Both are filthy.

Both have rejected Ben Johnson's plea for reinstatement.

34. Pamela Lee and a beach ball

Both inflatable.

Both have been chased by young boys at the beach.

Both have been batted around by Tommy Lee at a concert.

35. Bill Clinton and Juan Antonio Samaranch

Both have denied any wrongdoing.

Both refuse to resign.

Both take it under the table

(If you know what I mean).

36. George Michael and peaches

Both are fuzzy.

Neither talk to Andrew Ridgeley.

Both come in a can.

CONDITIONED RESPONSE

A list of responses to developments in news, sports, or entertainment. Often made from rejected monologue jokes, bits from our writers' stand-up acts, and the lips and ears of pigs.

1. **Ben Johnson's recent charity race**
   Canadian Olympic Association's response:
   "Oh, yeah. He's getting back in now."
   Donovan Bailey's response:
   "I'd like to thank Ben for making the "Race of the Century" look like a legitimate sporting event."
   Mike Tyson's response:
   "Great idea. I think my first comeback fight will be against a horse or a stock car."

2. **Oprah Winfrey's dazzling weight loss and makeover**
   Fan club response:
   "She gets more and more beautiful every year."
   Fashion industry response:
   "You'll be seeing her on a lot of magazine covers this year."
   Rosie O'Donnell's response:
   "Goddamn you, Oprah, we had a pact!"

3. Quebec's upcoming provincial election

Quebec separatists' response:

"A decisive victory will be the first step on the road to independence."

Quebec federalists' response:

"A win by Charest's Liberals will be in the best interest of all Québécois."

Rest of Canada's response:

"How do you say 'Rat's ass' in French?"

4. The success of the movie *Antz*

Critics' response:

"This is the kind of genius that inspires a genre."

Moviegoers' response:

"At last, something the whole family can enjoy."

Dung beetles' response:

"They star in a hit movie and all we get is a lousy ClearNet commercial just because people can't get past this 'dung' thing."

5. The British serial-killing doctor

Scotland Yard's response:

"Ninety is just scratching the surface. Who knows how many more victims there are."

British media's response:

"At ninety dead, this is definitely the largest mass murder case in the nation's history."

Dr. Jack Kevorkian's response:

"Ninety? He's gotta be on steroids.

6. Mary Kaye LeTourneau giving birth in prison

Public's response:

"It's a shame an innocent child has to suffer for the sins of its mother."

15-year-old lover's response:

"I'm counting the days until we are together as a family."

Babysitter's response:

"If I have to get a cavity search every time I come over here, I want six dollars an hour."

7. The ongoing Spraypec investigation

Opposition's response:

"This investigation is further proof that Chrétien's Liberals aren't fit to govern."

RCMP's response:

"If the results should find us liable, we will take full responsibility."

Pepper-sprayed students' response:

"It's good the investigation is under way, but is the re-enactment necessary?

8. Brian Mulroney's Order of Canada

Governor General's response:

"We know people will have objections, but we feel he deserves it."

Fellow Tories' response:

"This will rehabilitate him in the eyes of Canadians."

Satan's response:

"I realize I've made a mistake, but what can I do? — He won't take his soul back."

9. NBA lockout

Fans' response:

"Once again we're getting the short end of the stick."

Sports media's response:

"This work stoppage looks bad. It could last a long time."

WNBA's response:

"What's with all the flat-chested girls trying out for the teams?"

10. The Playboy Bunny 2000 search

Women's groups' response:

"Why perpetuate sexism into the next millennium?"

Playboy subscriber's response:

"Considering Playboy's high standards, this Bunny will be a knockout."

Juggs magazine's response:

"Send a photographer down there quick, there're sure to be rejects."

11. Clinton's sex scandal

Republican's response:

"It's a national disgrace that he abused the power of his office."

American people's response:

"We can't believe this happened in the White House."

Bob Guccione's Response:

"At this time I'd like to announce my candidacy for president."

12. The low Canadian dollar

Bank of Canada's response:

"An interest rate hike may be necessary."

Travel agent's response:

"Many of our Canadian customers have cancelled plans to travel abroad."

Jean Chrétien and Paul Martin's response:

"We've been playing golf all summer — we thought low numbers were good."

13. The box office smash *There's Something About Mary*

Movie industry's response:

"The film's success proves that low-budget comedies are alive and well."

Studio's response:

"Given what it cost to make, we're thrilled with the result."

Monica Lewinsky's response:

"That's so fake. It doesn't really make your hair go like that."

14. Russia's economic crisis

Financial experts' response:

"Despite the hardships, they must continue with market reform."

Political analysts' response:

"There's no question this fragile democracy is in jeopardy."

Communists' response:

"Don't blame us. We voted for oppressive dictatorship."

15. The Maple Leaf's move to the Air Canada Centre

Team's response:

"We hope this move will rejuvenate our organization."

Fans' response:

"Increased seating capacity means we have a better chance to score tickets."

Air Canada's response:

"Sorry about the mix up but we sent your equipment to the Saddledome."

16. *Open Mike*'s 1998 five-month summer vacation

Wayne Gretzky restaurant's response:

"They left this place a total pigsty. We're gonna have a long talk when they get back."

Comedy Network subscribers' response:

"Reruns on cable? What a shock."

Postal union's response:

"Only five months' vacation? Why don't they go on strike?"

17. Allegations that Bobby Hull made racial remarks

Bobby Hull's response:

"I was misquoted. Mr. Hitler was this century's most evil man."

Interviewing reporter's response:

"I stand by my story."

Marge Schott's response:

"Bobby Hull had some good ideas, but he went too far."

18. **The McGwire-Sosa home run record chase**

MLB commissioner Bud Selig's response:

"This couldn't come at a better time for baseball's image.

Baseball fans' response:

"With all that's going on in the world, it's great to have heroes we can believe in again."

Cal Ripkin's response:

"Excuse me. Longest-running consecutive games played streak still alive over here. Heeeeellooo."

19. **High-definition TV**

Electronics industry' response:

"Enhanced picture quality will create a huge demand."

Consumer advocates' response:

"The public should not be forced to replace existing TV sets."

Open Mike viewers, three years from now:

"It's like this guy is sucking right in the room with us."

20. **Jean Chrétien's snub of King Hussein's funeral**

Opposition's response:

"He has clearly embarrassed the nation."

King Hussein's response:

No response.

21. CBC Technicians strike

CBC management's response:

"We believe our offer is a fair one."

Striking CBC technicians' response:

"All this picketing outside gives us more time to smoke."

Response of viewers in remote regions of the country without cable or satellite whose one and only channel is CBC:

"Eh, we'll get by."

22. Theoren Fleury's trade to the Colorado Avalanche

Smart-ass Avalanche fans' response:

Five foot five? Guess he won't have to adjust to the altitude."

Theoren Fleury's response:

"I hope Denver has better dentists than Calgary."

23. Canadian domination of music industry

Doug and the Slugs' response:

"We're puttin' the band back together!"

24. Janitors' strike in Toronto schools

People who live near the schools' response:

"When you get ten janitors in a picket line, the noise from the keys is unbearable."

25. **Monica Lewinsky's two-hour Barbara Walters interview**

Viewers' response:

"It didn't reveal anything we don't already know."

White House response:

"We're focusing our energy on getting on with the nation's business."

Monica Lewinsky's response:

"I'm shocked and upset that my former friend Barbara Walters taped our private conversation without my knowledge."

26. **Monica Lewinsky admitting she considered killing herself by jumping off a balcony**

Her mother's response:

"It's tragic that this ordeal drove her to that point."

60 Minutes' response:

"We would have had no problem airing that."

Washington seismologist's response:

"You thought the scandal made an impact!"

27. **Dennis Rodman in L.A.**

Lakers fans' response:

"He's the spark this team needed."

Shaquille O'Neal's response:

"There's only room for one bad actor on this team."

Response of the guy in Chicago who used to spray-paint Rodman's head:

"I'm staying in Chicago. I got a job on a new show called The guy who used to spray-paint Dennis Rodman's head & Ebert.*"*

28. **Sun Media Corp laying off 160 employees nationwide**

Laid-off editor in chief's response:

"And we were worried The Toronto Star would lay us off!"

Laid-off science and health columnist's response:

"This is the human toll of big business mergers."

All eighteen Sunshine Girl photographers' response:

"Hey, we all got raises."

29. **B.C. Premier Glen Clark's home being raided by the RCMP**

Glen Clark's response:

"The facts will absolve me of any wrongdoing."

Opposition leader's response:

"It's high time this scandal-ridden premier step down."

Response of a well-respected child pornographer who lives next door:

"He's giving this neighbourhood a bad name."

30. **Takeover of Ontario convenience stores by a Quebec conglomerate**

Shareholders' response:

"The Quebec offer reflected fair market value for Beckers and Mac's Milk."

Customers' response:

"I hope this means lower prices on Vachon Cakes."

Quebec conglomerate's response:

"The stores were appealing because we don't have to worry about any employees there speaking English."

BULLARD'S BULLETS

A rapid-fire comment on a list of people, places, and things in the news. My least-favourite desk bit, this was originally conceived as a parody of those "hot topics" lists you see in *Entertainment Weekly* and various newspapers, but it often comes off more as a rip-off of those things.

1. **Lewinsky's videotaped testimony**
   I thought I was watching a Delta Burke screen test.

2. **Maple Leaf Gardens closing**
   Thirty years of failure and child abuse. Yeah, we'll miss that.

3. **Mike Bullard hosting the Junos**
   Everyone will be saying the same thing — Jason Priestley's really let himself go.

4. **Boris Yeltsin**
   The people behind death's door want you to stop ringing the bell and running away.

5. **The Pope's upcoming CD**
   I hear he's dropping by MuchMusic for an "Infallible and Interactive."

6. **The movie *Payback***
   I'd still like some "payback" for sitting through *Lethal Weapon 4*.

7. Y2K

On New Year's Eve, 1999, I'll be in a shelter eating Beefaroni out of a can. Just like every year.

8. Valentine's Day on Sunday

The office was closed, so I had to pass out raunchy heart candies in church.

9. Lesbians in tennis

Remind me to watch more doubles. If you know what I mean.

10. The movie *Life is Beautiful*

Slapstick in a death camp. Look for Robin Williams in *Patch Mengele*.

11. Pancakes

Always a treat.

12. Leafs torch-passing ceremony

I hope it wasn't touched by any of those losers from the eighties.

13. The budget surplus

No more excuses: Canadians *demand* a nuclear bomb.

14. Mark Patterson's sudden popularity

Now I've seen everything.

15. Gallagher cancellation

More wrestlers for *Open Mike*.

16. Bear hunt cancellation

I don't eat bear — but they better not cancel the cow hunt.

17. Y2K dangers

That's months away.

18. Mel Lastman's new beer

That reminds me: Don't drink and vote.

19. Former Nova Scotia Premier Gerald Regan's rape trial

No means no.

20. Lucien Bouchard

Ditto.

21. Meteor showers threatening the Earth's satellites

Great. I'll miss *Armageddon* on pay-per-view.

22. Brad Pitt's three-hour romantic comedy

Meet Joe Bored.

23. *The Waterboy* making millions

I think the Bills are overpaying that backup quarterback.

24. The collapse of Eaton's department stores

Just when I was gonna buy a new black and white Zenith TV.

25. Sarah McLachlan's copyright trial

You mean I have to pay my writers?

26. Peter Mansbridge marrying Cynthia Dale

I hear Knowlton Nash puked at the bachelor party.

27. Prince Charles turns fifty

Shouldn't he have a job by now?

28. Winnipeg electing a gay mayor
I hear he choreographed the Grey Cup half-time show.

29. Jean Charest
You didn't really sell your house in Ottawa, did you?

30. Roger Clemens's fifth Cy Young Award
What is that? I don't know.

31. Recall of toxic baby toys
The damage has been done. Let 'em play.

32. Reform uniting with the Tories
Like anyone'll vote for a party called the "ReformaTories."

33. Calista Flockhart
Look, anorexia is no joke. Next.

34. Ally McBeal's weight
She has to be thin, or who would care about her stupid problems?

35. Thirty shopping days until Xmas
So how many until Boxing Day?

36. Bouchard/Charest debate
Finally we know where they stand on these issues.

37. The guy on the subway who looks over your shoulder when you're reading the paper
Buy your own!

38. B.C. suing the tobacco industry
They need the money to support their heroin habit.

39. Alanis Morissette's new video

Hey, you can't do that on television.

40. NHL goal-scoring drought

Bigger nets, already.

41. Brian Orser's palimony suit

Flamer vs. Flamer.

42. Luciano Pavarotti's no show in Hamilton.

Must've been ten-cent wing night in Oakville.

Hey, Mike: I notice that the *Globe and Mail* lists all the other shows but not yours. They even list *Studio2*, which as far as I can tell isn't even a national show. As Orin might say, "What's up with that, Mike?"

CARL S., WHISTLER, B.C.

Carl, you have sent your e-mail to the wrong place. Because God knows I have asked my producers. I have asked my manager. I have asked my publicists. No one can tell me why we aren't in those listings. We don't even know who writes them. But to be fair, the *Globe* did include us in their listings once — when Jan Wong made her first visit. Now I love Jan Wong. Some of that celebrity know-how must have rubbed off on her because she makes a pretty good one herself. She's an excellent talk show guest. Not even Tom Green rattles that woman's cage. Although, now that I think of it, I don't think the *Globe* included Jan's second visit in their listings. Maybe they weren't as impressed as I was. Who knows? The *Globe* is a mysterious place, Carl. Frankly, I'm afraid of it and I think you should be too.

Hey, Mike: Do you drive a —? Because I was hitch-hiking on the QEW and I saw you and you didn't stop. Thanks a lot.

K. R.

Hitchhiking, it's incredible. It amazes me. I buy the car. I pay for the insurance. I pay for the gas. I pay for the upkeep. And then, let me see if I get this right, you come along and you think there's a reasonable assumption that I should come right up to where you are standing and take you where you want to go — for free? Why? Why would I do that? You answer me that!

Hey, Mike: Why are you so uncomfortable with guests who are bigger celebrities than you are? My father suggests that you have an inferiority complex. Is that it?

SUSAN N.

Susan? This is the third letter you've sent about me having problems. What's going on? Are you really mad at me or what? Have we dated?

Hey, Mike: Did you and Pat have fun as kids?

JOYCE, B.C.

Well fun is one word for it. I remember when one morning at six, my brother Pat and I decided to run away. When we got caught we said we went camping. We'd packed two kilograms of bacon and a suitcase. If we'd made the mistake of eating the bacon, I wouldn't be here to tell this story. Of course, what amazes me now is that we had two kilograms of bacon in the house, but that's what those days were like. Today, those two kilograms of bacon alone would be reason enough for Children's Aid to take us away.

Anyway, Pat and I got up, sneaked out of the house, and made our way towards the Rouge River Valley, near Don Mills. We'd left around six and my parents got up around eight, noticed we were gone, and calmly called the police. After we had made a camp, we came back down to the road and a police cruiser saw us. The officer asked if I was Mike Bullard and I replied, "Sorry. I'm not allowed to talk to strangers." He showed us his badge and said to get in the car. We said no. So we walked and he followed us the three kilometres home. When we got there my mother was waiting in the door and the cop said, "Look how worried your mother is." And I said, "Stick around." I knew her well enough to know that we were in big trouble. We never ran away again. I tried, but she just said, "Go ahead." It was no fun when I had her permission.

WHY I HATE SOME OF THE BEST MOVIES EVER MADE

The Wizard of Oz
Yeah, nice special effects. Those yellow brick road backdrops are so fake — look out, you four! You're about to skip into a wall.

Raging Bull
Starts out good. DeNiro is lean and mean in the first part, but by the end of the film he looks like crap. They should have paid someone to keep him away from the craft services table.

The Godfather
Everyone knows the real Mafia lives in Sudbury.

Pulp Fiction
I don't know who edited this, but a lot of the plot occurs out of sequence. Sloppy.

American Graffiti
In my opinion, Suzanne Somers was wasted.

Close Encounters of the Third Kind
A guy plays with his food, climbs to the top of a mountain, and watches a midget walk down a plank. Wake me up when they get to the flying bikes.

M*A*S*H
I saw this on video after I was familiar with the sitcom. A laugh track would have helped. Also, not enough Sergeant Zale.

Vertigo
Jimmy Stewart's kind of creepy in this one. I have no idea why it's considered a Christmas classic.

One Flew Over the Cuckoo's Nest
I don't know how much money was received from the JuicyFruit corporation, but product placement infuriates me.

Singin' in the Rain
If there's one thing I can't abide, it's co-ordinated optimists.

Hey, Mike: Sometimes I like to pretend I'm a mobster. I give my keys to my friends and ask them to start my car.

KELL

Sometimes I like to pretend I'm in the IRA. Let's get together.

Hey, Mike: Of all the letters you've received, what's the stupidest question ever asked?

John, the stupidest question is one we get constantly, and it always goes something like this actual e-mail:

Hello, Mr. Mike:
I think everybody who watches your show knows, that you have so called famous canadian people on like every show. Well if your going to get some good canadian talent why don't you give "Norm Macdonald", "Jim Carrey", "Pamela Anderson Lee", "Mike Meyers" or the guy in that commercial, (oh you know which one), a call to be on your show.

A LOYAL FAN,
BILLY M., RED DEER, ALBERTA

Our talent bookers spend about sixty hours a week, forty weeks a year, securing guests for the show. Anyone who thinks they are unaware of the advantages of booking Jim Carrey should not be allowed to drive or vote.

We've been lucky enough to have three out of five Kids in the Hall on our show, but apart from them, the Canadians who've struck it rich in the U.S. are not interested in doing a Canadian talk show. Part of the reason is that they don't live here. When they do come to Toronto, it's generally to visit with family and friends and not to do press of any kind.

When it comes time for big stars to promote their movies, even movies that were shot in Canada, they invariably go to L.A. and New York and maybe Chicago, and that's it. They're not picky about what shows they do — they'll talk to *Good Morning Moose Jaw*, as long as *GMMJ* sends someone to L.A. to do the interview. But this does nothing for us, because we need our guests to be in Toronto. Once, during our first season, I tried doing a satellite interview with Chris Rock, and it was a disaster because he couldn't react to our studio audience.

Guest unavailability is the number-one reason a made-in-Canada talk show has always been considered doomed. My brother Pat had a local show in Vancouver, but gave up on his dream of doing a national show because the guests just weren't around. We actually see it as something of an advantage that our guests, though lower-profile than Conan O'Brien's, are people you've never seen on a talk show before. We've all seen George Clooney and Richard Simmons a million times on a million different shows, but Pat McKenna and Tom Green made their talk show debuts on our show. The fact that we provide a genuine alternative is probably why the show works.

To recap, Billy: asking us to book massive stars is like me asking you to use proper spelling and grammar — it's just not a realistic goal.

Hey, Mike: You have all these great guests on your show (Dave Mustaine, Tim Owens, Glen Tipton, and Tommy Chong) but that's all they are ... guests. Why don't you ask them to perform on your show? You always have rotten, crappy bands performing and people from good bands sittin' there talking to ya. I'm sure Megadeth or Judas Priest wouldn't have minded doing a little number for you, and Tommy Chong could've done an act. My question is ... why?

KEEP UP THE GOOD WORK,
ERIC, NOVA SCOTIA

These people are simply look-alikes. Do you believe for a minute that the real Tommy Chong or Dave Mustaine would be caught dead on our show? Grow up!

Hey, Mike: I rarely write letters unless I am very ticked or very pleased with something. Today, I'm writing to say that I thought Mike's kiss was totally out of line. UNprofessional (regardless of whether the guest is male or female). Disgusting! And it made the guest uncomfortable.

I liked the show until now, but from now on, I'm not staying up to watch. I don't want this read out on air. Thank you for listening.

ALYSSA

I may have lost you, Alyssa, but I got the cover of *FAB*!

Hey, Mike: This is Taylor from Medicine Hat, Alberta. I'm fourteen and watch your show every day. My mom said that watching your show is a waste of time, and you probably drink varnish. Anyway, you are the most SPAWNtaneous comedian I've ever watched. Much like me and my friend John. We roam the school hallways in the morning looking for people to drive nuts. Their most common reply is "Are you two on crack?" then we reply, "No, but I enjoy a couple of paint chips in the morning." Although our best routine is going into a berserk rage of insanity, then calmly saying, "Yes, I am retarded and you are gawking at me." Tell the band they're the best and I hope to see this on the show. Mike, you're hilarious, try to keep up the reputation.

SINCERELY, TAYLOR

Yes, I'm quick-witted and sleep with fish.

Hey, Mike: Great show you got there. I'm happy to see you don't touch your nose every ten seconds because it was driving me nuts! Don't you think it's time to get some new guest chairs? The one's you have now suck.

YOUR PAL, STEVEN, VANCOUVER

Now that I'm off the coke, we may have money for new furniture.

Hey, Mike: I dunno if you guys know this, but you can hardly hear Mark's guitar when they play ... just thought I'd let you know ...

ROOT

This has contributed greatly to his job security.

Hey, Mike: Mark, Mark, your guitar solos rule. But the really weird thing is you remind me of Jimi Hendrix.

ANONYMOUS

This was the letter that made us sit up, take notice, and consider rehab for Mark.

Hey Mike, Orin, MAN, wicked bass lines, how the hell do you do it? Keep it up buddy, n.s. is in awe of the tunes.

ANONYMOUS

Even Orin couldn't figure this one out.

Hey, Mike: Tony, why do take shit from Mike all the time? All you ever do is smile and nod at his smart remarks. Stand up for yourself, son, and say something snarky back. Chances are he'll find it very amusing, and you won't get tossed. You are a very talented guy, and you don't deserve that shit! Good luck.

ZIGGY

Tony is currently on probation for looking me in the eye at a production meeting.

Hey, Mike: What is up with you and Orin always banging fists, it's weird. And Tony (I don't know if that's his name or not ... the guy that plays the piano), well he's pretty cool, but the coolest guy is you, Mike.

TREVOR, STELLARTON, NOVA SCOTIA
P.S. I DON'T KNOW IF I SPELLED ORIN'S NAME
RIGHT, BUT ANYWAYS, I LOVE YOUR HAIR.

Cooler than Tony? It doesn't get better than this.

Hey, Mike: I find myself dangerously close to sitting in a puddle of my own urine every night your show is on ... (reruns included) heh heh.

Keep up the stellar work ... I hope someday I'll make it to Toronto long enough to sit as a guest in your audience. You, your staff, and band blow away both those chumps on the east and west coast of the big-headed country to the south of us!

Thanks for the big laughs and the entertaining banter. Thanks in advance for the stuff to come.

MARK, TIMMINS, ONTARIO

We were flattered until upon further investigation we discovered that Mark is eighty-six years old and has no indoor plumbing.

Hey, Mike: I for one am rapidly tuning out on this show. The idea of a Canadian version of a late-night talk show is good, but you've got the wrong guy and wrong format. For example, the other night Mike basically did a bar-scene comic "picking on" the audience when talking to the couple where the guy was a personal trainer and his girlfriend was (I believe) a model. There are many such instances where this tactic is being used and in poor taste. It is fine to joke with an audience but to basically embarrass them the way he does is not professional.

Further, the way he interviews is also tainted in the same way.

So, as far as I'm concerned ... cut your losses!!! ... go to Plan B!!!

PETER

We broke into the files at CTV after receiving this e-mail and were shocked to discover that Plan B was, in fact, Peter. Nice try, pal.

Hey, Mike: Writers, on your September 28 show, you screwed up!! Jesus is on a Tim Horton's in Bras d'Or, Nova Scotia, which is on Cape Breton Island. This is a little bit of a drive from "outside Halifax" — about a four-and-a-half-to-five hour drive!

Jesus drives a Testarossa.

Hey, Mike: I have been watching your show now for about two weeks. I really like the band, and the girl who does the intro at the beginning of the show.

REGARDS, DAN, BARRIE, ONTARIO

P.S. I THOUGHT YOUR MOTHER WAS WONDERFUL LAST NIGHT AS WELL.

Sorry I got in the way.

Hey, Mike and fellow cronies: It's not often I take time out of my busy schedule of t.v. watching and other general lazy ass activities to comment on the work of others, but luckily this e-mail crap maximizes my laziness. First, I would like to say that you are a sadistic, self-centred, opinionated prick, but it's fortunate that I also share such qualities and tune in regularly. Power to those who speak their mind. I have a few complaints, though; first, I feel as though you hold back at times, not

realizing that the audience is there for your punishment. If there is a skanky crack-whore in the front row, LET IT BE KNOWN. If your band leader sidekick needs to replace his "MC Hammer" glass, let him know. I realize that even you have to tiptoe around the tight-ass network executives, but show some signs of a spine.

Secondly, do something with your hands. Half the time you're wiping your nose like you just did a couple of coke rails in between commercials, the other half of the time it looks like you're wringing your hands with more guilt then a molesting Catholic priest. I know there can be long periods of silence during your monologue but ease up. Any way, with no fear of any actual comedic retribution I will inclose my name. Take your best shot, fat boy.

ANGUS B., OTTAWA
AKA ANGUS "THE E-MAIL ASSASSIN" B.,
FORMERLY OF KING'S TOWN

I'm not messing with any e-mailer who has an alias.

Hey, Mike: Did you really write this whole book?

ANONYMOUS

In the position that I am in I can't write a book like this by myself. Putting a book out is like putting a show out. It takes a lot of people. I argued with the publisher and they finally agreed to let me acknowledge my co-workers as long as I put it at the end of the book. Thanks to my editor Maya Mavjee who started this whole mess and then whittled it down from 5000 pages. How she carried it from my house to her office is beyond me. She only weighs 90 pounds. And thanks to my publicist Adrienne Ball, providing that 25,000 people are now holding copies of this book. Thanks to Alex Pugsley for the coffee and the sandwiches.

The other people involved are the same people who help me get to air every night. My manager Howard Lapides negotiated the deal. My producer Al Magee came up with the idea of answering the e-mail. My co-producer Laura MacDonald co-ordinated everyone involved and wrote along with my regular writers Greg Eckler, Rob Ross and my field producer Sean Tweedley. And desk bits from the show would have been originally written by myself, Greg, Rob and head writer Lawrence Morgenstern and produced by Al. So I would like to thank those who made $5000 less than I did, but $2500 more when you consider management fees. Thanks again Howard.

Mike Bullard